THE ARISTOCRAT OF GAMES!

The game of chess is the most gratifying and intriguing pastime ever invented by man. This new book is the perfect introduction to the "royal" game. Written by Fred Reinfeld, America's foremost chess authority, it presents an easy-to-understand digest of all the basic rules and fundamentals of play. Unraveling a game renowned for its complexities, CHESS IN A NUTSHELL is a masterpiece of condensation and simplification.

FRED REINFELD has been one of the contributing editors of *Chess Review* since it was founded, in 1933. He has more than fifty chess books to his credit. He has also been on the staff of New York University as an instructor in chess. While still in his teens, Mr. Reinfeld became Intercollegiate Chess Champion and has been victorious over many renowned opponents.

Books by Fred Reinfeld

Chess in a Nutshell
Chess is an Easy Game

Published by POCKET BOOKS

Most Pocket Books are available at special quantity discounts for bulk purchases for sales promotions, premiums or fund raising. Special books or book excerpts can also be created to fit specific needs.

For details write the office of the Vice President of Special Markets, Pocket Books, 1230 Avenue of the Americas, New York, New York 10020.

FRED REINFELD

CHESS
in a nutshell

PUBLISHED BY POCKET BOOKS NEW YORK

POCKET BOOKS, a division of Simon & Schuster, Inc.
1230 Avenue of the Americas, New York, N.Y. 10020

Copyright © 1958 by Fred Reinfeld

Published by arrangement with Doubleday & Company, Inc.

ISBN: 0-671-49405-8

First Pocket Books printing March, 1960

30   29   28   27

POCKET and colophon are registered trademarks
of Simon & Schuster, Inc.

Printed in the U.S.A.

Contents

INTRODUCTION

OF ALL the major games, chess is the most popular, the most widespread, and the oldest. It has a literature more extensive than that devoted to all other games put together.

Part of the lure of chess lies in its tantalizing wealth of possibilities. Chess, it has been said, "is as much a mystery as women." A great master, when asked to explain why the game had fascinated him for more than half a century, replied that chess, "like love, like music, has the power to make men happy."

The search for improvement in one's chess-playing ability never comes to an end. There is always more to learn, more to admire, more to enjoy. Thus, chess gives us an endless vista of new experiences, new pleasures. It lifts our spirits out of the dullness of everyday living. More than a thousand years ago, Mu'tazz, the son of a Caliph of Baghdad, wrote that chess "yields us, when we need them most, companions in our loneliness."

An unfortunate prejudice that keeps some people away from chess is the popular belief that only a mental giant can play chess well. This is by no means the case.

Playing chess is a specialized skill which can be developed by training and practice. Everyone knows of exceedingly able specialists in all sorts of fields who are quite ordinary people outside their specialty. This applies to the great chessmasters as well, who are rarely exceptional outside of chess.

In fact, some of these great players are often disappointingly limited individuals. James Mortimer dismissed them bluntly in his pompous Victorian prose when he observed tartly that "it will be cheering to know that many people are skillful chessplayers, though in many instances, their brains, in a general way, compare unfavorably with the cogitative faculties of a rabbit." As far as Mortimer was concerned, these chessmasters were not even on the level of a "dumb bunny."

Another important point to remember is this: to enjoy chess, you don't have to be a great master; you only have to be a little better than your opponents. And since your opponents will just be run-of-the-mill players, you don't have to set your sights too high.

What is important, though, is to get off to a good start—to have a clear picture of the basic rules of the game. Then you can go on to learn the chess notation, so that you can record your games (if you wish), and play over games from books—in order to improve your game, or merely to enjoy beautiful, artistic chess.

By familiarizing yourself with the relative value of the different pieces, you take a big step forward in im-

proving your play. Most players who have never read a chess book are baffled by this simple but vitally important relationship, and thus they lose many games which they should never have lost.

Again, the aspiring chessplayer takes a big step forward when he gets a systematic grasp of the opening systems—their basic ideas, their classifications, their objectives. In the middle game and endgame, too, concentration on a few leading concepts takes much of the vague guesswork out of chess and helps the average player to plan, to foresee, to parry, to bring games to a victorious conclusion.

This book is not intended to transform you into a chess expert. The intention is, rather, to give you the minimum of information and counsel you need to play a fair game with confidence and enjoyment. In short, this book gives you "chess in a nutshell."

—FRED REINFELD

CHAPTER I

The Basic Rules of Chess

THE BOARD AND MEN

CHESS is played by two opponents on a chessboard made up of 64 squares.

Squares—These squares are arranged in eight vertical rows and eight horizontal rows.

The squares are alternately light and dark. Regardless of their actual color, the light squares are always referred to as "white" squares, and the dark squares, as "black" squares.

Before setting up the chessmen, place the board so that the righthand corner square nearest each player is a white square.

Files—The vertical rows of squares—those running from one player's side to the other player's side—are called "files."

Ranks—The horizontal rows of squares—those at right angles to the files—are called "ranks."

Diagonals—There is still another pattern of squares. It is called a "diagonal," and is made up of a series of squares which touch only at their corners. Each diagonal is made up exclusively of white squares or exclusively of black squares.

Chessmen—Each player has the following forces at the beginning of a game:

A King
A Queen
Two Rooks (or "Castles")
Two Knights
Two Bishops
Eight Pawns

THE OPENING POSITION

The position of the chessmen at the beginning of the game is shown in Diagram 1.

The term "chess piece" or "piece" refers to all the chessmen other than the Pawns. Thus, Rooks and Knights are pieces, but a Pawn is just a Pawn.

To distinguish the chessmen on each side, one set of chessmen is light-colored and the opposition is dark. The first set is called the "White" forces and the second group, the "Black" forces.

The player who has the White chessmen is referred to as "White." The player who has the Black chessmen is referred to as "Black."

In chess diagrams (*see* Diagram 1) the White forces are set out at the bottom, while the Black forces are set out at the top.

Diagram 1

BLACK

WHITE

Position of the Chessmen

The Rooks, which look like medieval towers, are placed in the four corners. Next to them are the Knights, represented by horses' heads. Then, still continuing toward the center, are the Bishops, which look like a bishop's miter.

The Queens are placed on one of the remaining empty squares on White's first rank and on Black's first rank. Remember the rule of *"Queen on color."* The White Queen goes on a white square; the Black Queen goes on a black square.

Thus, White's King goes on a black square. The Black King goes on a white square.

It is important to fix the position of the King and Queen carefully. (Inexperienced players have a distressing habit of placing the King and Queen on the wrong squares.)

The King is always the tallest piece in any set of chessmen, and can be recognized in diagrams by the small cross on top. (In most chess sets, the King will generally be topped by a cross.) White places his King on the remaining empty square on his first rank (*see* Diagram 1). Black places *his* King on the remaining empty square on his first rank.

In Diagram 1 the White Rooks face the Black Rooks on the same files (these are known as the "Rook files"). The White Knights face the Black Knights on the

Diagram 1*a*

BLACK

WHITE

Knight files. The White Bishops face the Black Bishops on the Bishop files. The White King faces the Black King on the King file. And lastly, the White Queen faces the Black Queen on the Queen file.

All that remains now is to place the Pawns on their proper squares. White's Pawns are placed on their second rank, in front of his pieces. Black's Pawns are placed on *his* second rank, in front of his pieces. This completes the situation shown in Diagram 1*a*—the standard opening position.

RULES OF MOVING

White always makes the first move.

The players move alternately.

Only one move can be made at a time.

A move is completed when one chessman has been transferred from one square to another. Only one chessman can be moved at a time. (One exception, known as "castling," is described on pages 27–34.)

No chessman except the Knight (pages 14–17) can leap over squares occupied by its own or enemy forces. Castling is the only other exception to this rule.

Each chessman except the Knight can move in only one direction at a time.

Only one chessman can occupy a given square at a time.

CAPTURING

Chessmen capture by displacement—that is, by removing the captured enemy unit from the square it occupies and replacing it on the same square with the capturing chessman. This is all considered one move, although two chessmen are handled in the process. (Capturing *en passant* [in passing] is the only exception to this rule. It is described on pages 21–24.)

Only one capture can be made at a time.

COMPULSORY MOVES AND CAPTURES

Each chessman is moved and captures according to the powers laid down for it in the rules of chess.

All chess moves are optional, with the following exceptions:

If a player's King is under attack (threatened with capture), then that player must make a move that ends the attack. If the only way to end the attack is to capture the attacking enemy chessman, then that capture must be executed.

Making a move is a duty as well as a privilege. A player can never skip his turn to play. If he has only one possible move and it is obviously disadvantageous, he must play it anyway.

PROHIBITED MOVES AND CAPTURES

If a player contemplates a move that would expose his King to capture, then he cannot make that move.

If a player contemplates a capture that would expose his King to capture, then he cannot make his intended capture.

HOW CHESSMEN MOVE AND CAPTURE

KING MOVES AND CAPTURES

The King is the most important piece in chess. This is explained under "Check" and "Checkmate" (pages 34–40).

The King can move in any direction to an adjacent square which is not within the capturing range of any enemy chessman. (The King can move only one square at a time, except when castling, pages 27–34). The

Diagram 2

BLACK

WHITE

King can capture any hostile unit on an adjacent square which is not within the capturing range of an enemy chessman.

In Diagram 2 the White King can make any one of eight possible moves, each indicated by crosses.

The Black King, in the same diagram, can choose any of the following:

1. It can capture the White Knight.

2. It can move one square horizontally (indicated by a cross).

3. It can move one square vertically (indicated by a cross).

When the King makes a capture, the captured unit is removed from the board and the King replaces it on the same square.

Other information about the King appears under these headings:

Compulsory Moves and Captures (page 6)
Prohibited Moves and Captures (pages 6–7)
Check (pages 34–40)
Checkmate (pages 34–40)
Stalemate (pages 44–45)
Castling (pages 27–34)

IMPORTANCE OF THE KING

At this point it will suffice to say that a game of chess is won by attacking the hostile King in such a way that no matter what the opponent replies, *his King cannot escape from attack*. The King is not captured—it is enough to produce a position in which it is attacked and *cannot escape*.

QUEEN MOVES AND CAPTURES

The Queen is the most powerful piece in chess. Its moving and capturing range is bigger than that of any other chess unit.

The Queen's move is an enlarged version of the King's move. The Queen can move to any empty square of the file or rank or diagonals on which it is placed. In other words, the Queen can move vertically, horizontally, or diagonally.

Diagram 3

BLACK

WHITE

In Diagram 3, the Queen can move to any of the squares marked with a cross. Although the Queen has a choice of many different squares, it can move in only one direction and to one specific square on any one move.

The Queen can make only one capture at a time.

When the Queen captures, the captured hostile unit is removed from its square and replaced by the capturing Queen.

Diagram 3a

BLACK

WHITE

The Queen can capture any hostile piece located within its moving range. The Queen captures the same way it moves—either vertically, horizontally, or diagonally.

In Diagram 3a the White Queen has a choice of cap-

turing the Black Bishop (by a vertical move) *or* the
Black Knight (by a horizontal move) *or* the Black Pawn
(by a diagonal move).

ROOK MOVES AND CAPTURES

The Rook is the next most powerful piece after the
Queen. The Rook can move and capture vertically *or*
horizontally.

Diagram 4 shows how the Rook moves on files or
ranks. The Rook can move in only one direction at a
time.

Diagram 4

BLACK

WHITE

In Diagram 4 the White Rook can move to *any one*
of the squares marked with a cross. It can capture the
Black Pawn (vertical move) *or* the Black Knight

(horizontal move). The Rook can capture only one unit at a time.

When the Rook captures, the captured hostile unit is removed from its square and replaced by the capturing Rook.

The Rook, like the Queen, is obstructed by the presence of hostile or friendly units that stand in its way.

One other aspect of Rook play is noted under the heading of "Castling" (pages 27–34).

BISHOP MOVES AND CAPTURES

The Bishop has the one power of the Queen which the Rook lacks. That is, the Bishop can move only on diagonals. It captures the same way as it moves. The Bishop's moving and capturing powers are shown in Diagram 5.

In Diagram 5, the White Bishop can move to *any one* of the squares marked with a cross. The White Bishop can also capture the Black Queen *or* the Black Knight *or* the Black Pawn.

However, the White Bishop cannot capture the Black Rook, as the Bishop's path is obstructed by the White Pawn on that diagonal.

Like the King and Queen and Rook, the Bishop can move in only one direction at a time. If it has a choice of several captures, it can make only one capture at a time.

When the Bishop captures, the captured hostile unit

is removed from its square and replaced by the capturing Bishop.

One other interesting aspect of the Bishop's move remains to be noted. Whereas the files and ranks are made up of alternating white and black squares, each diagonal is made up of squares of the same color.

Diagram 5

BLACK

WHITE

It follows that each Bishop is limited to squares of one color. Each player has one Bishop that travels only on black squares and one Bishop that travels only on white squares.

Since the Bishop captures the same way as it moves, all hostile units placed on the other color are safe from attack by the Bishop. All units on black squares, for example, are immune to threat or capture by a hostile Bishop that moves on white squares.

It is vital to maneuver a Bishop so as to extract the utmost from its mobility. Furthermore, it can be very useful to operate with both Bishops, for this "Bishop-pair" has potential access to all the squares of both colors. This is a fine point that often escapes the inexperienced player's attention.

KNIGHT MOVES AND CAPTURES

The Knight's move has many interesting facets. Handling this piece skillfully is the hallmark of a good player, who achieves many victories thereby. Mastering the Knight's move takes a little practice, but it is well worth the trouble.

The Knight's move is illustrated in Diagram 6.

In Diagram 6 the White Knight can move to *any one* of the squares marked with a cross.

What is the principle of the Knight's move? At first glance it looks mysterious, for, unlike the King, the Queen, the Rook, or the Bishop, the Knight does *not* move in a straight line.

The fact is that the Knight moves in two directions in one move. First the Knight moves one square sideways (to the right or left)—or else vertically (forward or backward). Then, *still moving away from the square it has just left,* the Knight moves one square diagonally.

The end result is a Knight move in the shape of a

capital *L*. The Knight can move to only one of its available squares at a time.

The Knight's ultimate destination will depend on:

1. *Which direction it moves one square sideways or vertically, and*

2. *Which direction it then moves one square diagonally.*

Diagram 6

WHITE

Here is a feature of the Knight move which it is useful to remember. If the Knight moves from a white square, it will land on a black square. If the Knight moves from a black square, it will end up on a white square.

As to capturing: if a Black unit were located on each

of the squares marked with a cross in Diagram 6, the Knight could capture *any one* of those Black units. In other words, the Knight captures the same way it moves.

A second diagram will make this quite clear. In Diagram 7, then, White's Knight can capture *any one* of the Black Pawns.

Diagram 7

BLACK

WHITE

What about the White Pawns in Diagram 7? They rule out two of the Knight's possible moves. (To see which two, turn back to Diagram 6.) Like all the other chessmen, *the Knight cannot move to a square already occupied by one of its own units.*

Another important feature of the Knight's move: it can leap over its own or enemy units when making

moves or captures. Thus, in Diagram 7, the White
Knight, in capturing any of the Black Pawns, can leap
over the Black Queen or Rook, or over the White
Queen and Bishop.

There is no contact whatever between the Knight
and the other units on the intermediate squares of its
move. It cannot capture hostile units on these intermediate squares; nor is it obstructed by its own units
on these intermediate squares.

The Knight's Move Summarized

The discussion of Diagrams 6 and 7 can be summed
up as follows:

1. The Knight's move is shown in Diagram 6. Its
capturing method is shown in Diagram 7.

2. The Knight's move is always of the same length.

3. Like the other chessmen, the Knight cannot move
to a square occupied by one of its own units.

4. Unlike the other chessmen, the Knight can leap
over its own or enemy forces to move or capture.

PAWN MOVES AND CAPTURES

The Pawn differs in four ways from the other chessmen:

1. The Pawn moves in only one direction: *forward*.
As it cannot retreat, Pawn moves must be chosen with
care.

2. The Pawn does not capture in the same way that it moves.

3. Under certain conditions, the Pawn can be converted into a much more powerful unit.

4. The Pawn has the power of capturing *en passant* (in passing)—given the proper setting (pages 21–24).

Standard Pawn Moves

The Pawn's standard move is to advance one vacant square straight ahead in its file.

However, if the Pawn has not yet been moved and is still on its original square on the second rank (as in Diagram 1 or 1*a*), a player has the option of moving it one *or* two vacant squares straight ahead.

This applies not only to the opening position, but to *any* stage of the game. As long as a Pawn remains unmoved, it has the option of moving one *or* two vacant squares straight ahead.

Pawn Moves Illustrated

In studying Pawn moves from diagrams, remember that White Pawns move toward the Black side, and that Black Pawns move toward the White side.

Diagram 8 illustrates several rules of Pawn play.

Since the White Pawn at the reader's extreme right is still on its original square, it has the option of advancing one *or* two squares.

Diagram 8

BLACK

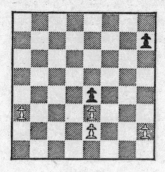

WHITE

The Black Pawn on the same file has the same option. None of the three Pawns on the center file can move: none of them has a vacant square in front of it. (No capture is possible here because Pawns do not capture straight ahead.)

The White Pawn at the reader's left (Diagram 8) has already moved from its original square on White's second rank. Therefore it can only move one square straight ahead.

Pawn Captures Illustrated

Pawns capture *diagonally* on the forward adjacent squares to the right or left. This is illustrated in Diagram 9.

Diagram 9

BLACK

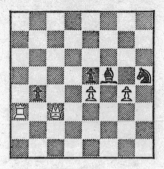

WHITE

In Diagram 9 the White Pawns have the following moving and capturing possibilities:

1. The White Pawn at the reader's right can (*a*) advance one square straight ahead or (*b*) capture the Black Knight or (*c*) capture the Black Bishop.

2. The White Pawn on the center file can capture the Black Bishop. This Pawn cannot move straight ahead, because its path is blocked by a Black Pawn directly in front of it. Nor can the White Pawn capture this Black Pawn, because Pawns do not capture straight ahead.

In Diagram 9 the Black Pawns have the following moving and capturing possibilities:

1. The Black Pawn at the reader's left can (*a*) ad-

vance one square straight ahead or (*b*) capture the
White Rook or (*c*) capture the White Queen.

2. The remaining Black Pawn has no move. It cannot advance, as its path is obstructed; and it cannot
capture the White Pawn in front of it.

Capturing En Passant *Summarized*

The elements involved in this special form of Pawn
capture are as follows:

1. Only a Pawn can capture *en passant*.

2. Only a Pawn can be captured *en passant*.

3. The Pawn that is eventually to be captured must
be on its second rank.

4. The Pawn that is to do the capturing must be on
its fifth rank.

5. The Pawns must be on adjacent files.

6. The Pawn that is to be captured *en passant* advances two squares.

7. In reply, the opponent's Pawn captures the first
Pawn *as if the latter had advanced only one square.*

Capturing En Passant *Illustrated*

Diagram 10 shows the typical situation for *en passant*
capture. White has a Pawn on his second rank, and
Black has a Pawn on his fifth rank on an adjacent file.

If White were to advance his Pawn *one* square, Black
could capture the White Pawn with his own Pawn. This
would be a forward diagonal capture on an adjacent

Diagram 10 (*White to play*)

BLACK

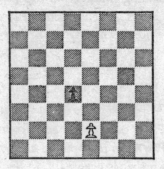

WHITE

square—the standard method of Pawn capture. (The resulting position is pictured in Diagram 12.)

Diagram 11 (*Black to play*)

BLACK

WHITE

But, in the position of Diagram 10, White actually advances his Pawn two squares. The resulting situation (Diagram 11) makes an *en passant* capture possible.

Now the Black Pawn can capture the White Pawn *en passant*. This means that Black's Pawn captures White's Pawn as if the latter had advanced only one square. The resulting position appears in Diagram 12.

Diagram 12 (*after* en passant *capture*)

BLACK

WHITE

En Passant *Capture Optional*

Capturing *en passant* is optional. When a player has the opportunity to capture, he may act on it or ignore it. However, if the opportunity is not seized at the first opportunity, then the *en passant* capture cannot be made subsequently.

There are two situations in which a compulsory feature is involved.

1. If a player's King is under attack and the only way to extricate the King is by an *en passant* capture, then that capture *must* be made.

2. If a player has an opportunity for *en passant* capture which would expose his King to attack, then he cannot make the capture.

PAWN PROMOTION

When a player advances one of his Pawns to the very end of a file, he replaces the Pawn—must replace it— with a new Queen *or* a new Rook *or* a new Bishop *or* a new Knight of the same color. (He cannot replace the Pawn with a new King.)

Diagram 13 (*White to play*)

BLACK

WHITE

As shown on pages 9–11, the Queen is the strongest of all the chess forces. Consequently it is customary to take a new Queen. The process is known as "promoting" a Pawn, or "queening" a Pawn. Diagram 13 shows how it is done.

White advances his Pawn one square to his last rank, removes the Pawn, and replaces it with a White Queen. (He could also have chosen a Rook or a Knight or a Bishop.) The advance of the Pawn, its removal from the board, and its replacement by the new Queen are all considered part of a single move.

Now it is Black's turn. He advances his Pawn to the last row and replaces it with a Black Queen. The position of Diagram 13 has been transformed into the position of Diagram 14.

Diagram 14 (*after Pawn promotion*)

BLACK

WHITE

Questions About Pawn Promotion

Some players believe that a new Queen cannot be obtained by promotion if the original Queen is still on the board. This is incorrect. A player can promote to a new Queen as often as his Pawns reach the last row. Similarly, he can promote to a Rook or a Knight or a Bishop even if the original pieces are still on the board.

Other players wonder whether the newly promoted piece can start functioning at once. The answer is that in order to move or capture, the new piece must wait until the player's next turn.

There is one exception to this rule. If the new piece attacks the hostile King from the promotion square, that attack must be parried at once by the opponent. (The reason for this is clear from the discussion of "Check," pages 34–40.)

Where does the new piece come from? It does not come from the pieces on the board, for in that case there would be no net gain in Pawn promotion. The new piece comes from the stock of pieces that have already been captured and removed from the board in previous play.

If the desired piece is not available from this source, it may be necessary to retain the promoted Pawn and provide it with some distinguishing sign of its new status—for example, fasten a rubber band around it.

When available, a Rook placed upside down is often used for a new Queen.

What is the importance of Pawn promotion? Why is it desirable? Pawn promotion greatly increases the force at a player's disposal. If by means of Pawn promotion he has two Queens against his opponent's single Queen, he has an advantage in material that is equivalent to winning the opposing Queen for nothing in return. Successful Pawn promotion almost invariably assures victory, as will be explained in Chapter 6.

CASTLING

"Castling" is the name of a unique kind of move. Its object is to get the King to a well-protected refuge where it will be comparatively difficult for the opposing

Diagram 15 (*before Castling*)

BLACK

WHITE

forces to menace this all-important piece. (For the importance of the King, *see* "Checkmate," pages 36–37.)

Castling is the only occasion in chess when a player is permitted to move two pieces, with the double move counting as only a single move.

The two pieces that are moved in Castling are the King and one of the Rooks. Diagram 15 shows the skeleton setup before Castling.

King-side Castling

King-side Castling occurs when White castles with his King and with the White Rook at the right of his King; or when Black castles with his King and with the Black Rook at the left of his King.

Diagram 16 (*after King-side Castling*)

BLACK

WHITE

To castle King-side, White moves the King two squares to the right, and then places the nearest White Rook at the immediate left of the new position of his King (*see* Diagram 16).

When Black castles King-side, he moves his King two squares to his left, and then places the nearest Black Rook at the immediate right of the new position of his King (*see* Diagram 16).

Queen-Side Castling

To castle Queen-side, White moves his King two squares to the left, and then places the nearest White Rook at the immediate right of his King's new position (*see* Diagram 17).

When Black castles Queen-side, he moves his King

Diagram 17 (*after Queen-side Castling*)

BLACK

WHITE

two squares to his right, and then places the nearest
Black Rook at the immediate left of his King's new
position (*see* Diagram 17).

Requirements for Castling

There are three basic conditions that must be satisfied before Castling is feasible.

1. The King must not have been moved previously
in the game.

2. The Rook which is to take part in Castling must
not have been moved previously in the game.

3. The squares between the King and Rook involved
in Castling must be vacant.

Conditions 1 and 2 are illustrated in Diagram 18.

Diagram 18

BLACK

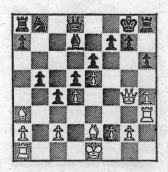

WHITE

In the position of Diagram 18, Black has moved his King and therefore he can never castle.

White can never castle King-side because he has moved the Rook needed for that purpose. However, White may castle Queen-side with his other Rook if he wishes to.

When Castling Is Impossible

Castling is *temporarily* impossible under the following conditions:

1. If a player's King is under attack, he cannot castle. Later on, however, if all the conditions are suitable, he can castle.

2. If any of the squares between a player's King and one of his Rooks is occupied, he cannot castle with that Rook. However, if the squares become vacant later on, he can castle then if all the other requirements have been met.

3. Castling is impossible if the King has to pass over a square controlled by enemy pieces. (On the other hand, note that a Rook can pass over squares controlled by enemy pieces.) However, if this control disappears later on, castling will then become feasible if all the other circumstances are favorable.

4. Castling is impossible if it involves placing the King on a square controlled by an enemy unit. If this condition disappears later on and all the other conditions are satisfactory, then it will be possible to castle.

Diagram 19 illustrates some of the prohibitions on castling.

Diagram 19 (*White to play*)

BLACK

WHITE

White's King is being attacked by a Black Knight and must be extricated at once. Since the King is under attack, White cannot castle *at this point*. He may be able to castle later on.

If White's King were not under attack now, he could castle King-side, as the squares between his King and the White Rook on the right are vacant. But he could not castle Queen-side, as one of the squares between his King and the White Rook on the left is occupied.

If White now moves his King in order to escape the attack by the Knight, then he can never castle.

And finally, if White captures the attacking Knight

with his white-square Bishop, then Black's Queen captures the White Bishop in turn. Now it is still impossible for White to castle King-side, as his King would have to pass over a square commanded by Black's Queen.

Diagram 20 illustrates another situation in which castling is impossible.

Diagram 20 (*White to play*)

BLACK

WHITE

White would like to castle King-side. He cannot do so because Black's black-square Bishop commands the square on which White's King would land in Castling.

Thus, White is unable to castle; but this disability need not be permanent. If he can remove the Black Bishop, or if it leaves the diagonal, or if the diagonal becomes blocked—if any of these things happens, White will be able to castle after all.

To close this section on castling, here is a summary of the conditions that make castling permanently impossible:

1. The King has moved previously.
2. Both Rooks have moved previously.
3. One Rook has moved previously, making it impossible to castle with that Rook. If the other Rook has not moved, however, it is still possible to castle with the second Rook.

CHECK AND CHECKMATE

CHECKS AND HOW THEY ARE ANSWERED

Any move that attacks a hostile King is known as a "check." As soon as a King is checked, this piece must get out of check immediately.

There are three ways for a player to get out of check:

1. By capturing the hostile unit that is giving check.
2. By interposing one of his own units on the line of attack between the checking unit and his own King. (This method cannot be used against checks by a Knight or by a Pawn.)
3. By moving his King to a square where it will no longer be within the attacking range of the hostile pieces.

All three ways of escaping from check are shown in the play that follows Diagram 21.

Diagram 21 (*Black to play*)

BLACK

WHITE

White's Queen is checking the Black King. Black must get out of check at once.

The simplest way for Black to do this is to capture White's Queen with his Bishop. That would put an immediate end to the check.

Another acceptable move for Black (as far as satisfying the laws of chess is concerned) is for him to retreat his Bishop to the square directly in front of the Black King, thus putting an end to the check. This is known as "interposing" to a check.

Finally, Black can get out of the check by moving his King—either one square sideways or one square diagonally. (Playing the Black King *forward* one square, however, would not get it out of check, as the King would still be under attack from the White Queen.)

Note that while the King is the only chessman that is subject to check, it is also the only chessman that cannot give check.

Announcing Check

It is conventional to announce "Check!" This is permissible and may even be advisable, but the rules do not require it.

CHECKMATE

Checkmate is the basic objective in a game of chess— to attack the hostile King in such a manner that he cannot escape no matter what the player does.

This means that the King is in check, and that it is impossible (*a*) to capture the checking unit or (*b*) to interpose against the check or (*c*) to move the King out of check. When none of these resources are available, the King is checkmated; the game is won by the player who has engineered the checkmate.

Diagram 22 illustrates a checkmate position.

Black is checkmated; White has won the game.

All the elements of checkmate are present:

1. White's Queen gives check.
2. Black cannot capture the Queen.

3. Black cannot interpose to the check.

4. Black cannot move his King out of check. (All the moves available to the Black King are in the capturing range of the White pieces.)

Diagram 22 (*Black is checkmated*)

BLACK

WHITE

Since checkmate is the goal of every game of chess, it follows that the King is of infinite value and that a player must at all times be very solicitous about shielding his King from any menacing attack.

OTHER FEATURES OF CHECK AND CHECKMATE

A player can never move his King into check, nor can he make a move that would submit his King to attack.

If the King is attacked, he cannot be allowed to remain in check. If, with the best will in the world, the player cannot get his King out of check, he has been checkmated.

The checkmated King is never actually captured, nor is it physically removed from the board. It's enough that the King is in a position from which it cannot escape.

Resigning

In practice, a player does not always wait to be checkmated when he realizes his position is hopeless. Instead, he often "resigns"—concedes defeat. Resignation has exactly the same significance as being checkmated.

As to what constitutes a hopeless position, see the section on relative values (pages 66–74) and also the chapters on winning methods and endgame play.

Discovered Check

A discovered check comes into being when a unit moves off a line and uncovers ("discovers") a check by another unit which *does not move*. (This differs from most checks, which come about by moving a unit to a square from which it gives check.)

Any chess unit can move aside to open up the line of attack by another unit of the same color. But only a Queen, a Rook, or a Bishop can give a discovered check merely by standing still.

Diagram 23 illustrates the point.

Diagram 23 (*White to play*)

BLACK

WHITE

In Diagram 23 White gives a discovered check with his Queen by capturing the Black Knight with his Rook.

Discovered checks can be extremely powerful, partly because they often come as a surprise to an unwary opponent, and partly because the uncovering piece can often make a valuable capture as it exposes the hostile King to a discovered check.

Double Check

This is a particularly devastating form of discovered check. In the case of double check, the uncovering unit also gives check as it unmasks the line of attack by a second piece.

This is what happens in the position of Diagram 23 if White captures the Black Rook with his own Rook. In that case, the White Queen's line of attack is opened up, enabling the Queen to give a discovered check. But in addition White's Rook, by capturing Black's Rook, is also giving check. So White gives *double check,* with his Queen and Rook.

Whereas theoretically there are three ways to escape an ordinary check, there is only one way to escape a double check, and that is to move the King out of check.

In Diagram 23, for example, after White's Rook captures Black's Rook with double check, Black's Knight cannot capture the White Queen, for White's Rook would still be giving check. Nor can Black's Knight capture the White Rook, for then White's Queen would still be giving check.

Nor can Black interpose his Bishop between his King and the White Rook, for then White's Queen would still be giving check.

As a matter of fact, in this particular instance Black cannot even escape by moving his King—for any King move would still leave that piece inside the capturing range of some White unit. Thus the double check has forced checkmate; the game is over: White has won.

DRAWN GAMES

A draw is a game in which neither side wins. In a tournament, a player who wins a game is credited with a point. The player who loses gets a zero. If the game is a draw, each player receives half a point. There are various ways in which a draw can come about, and they are dealt with in the following sections.

Draw by Agreement

The game is declared drawn *if both players agree to call the game a draw*. This result holds even though one of the players has a winning position. Mutual consent, freely given, establishes the result. As a rule, games are abandoned as drawn when neither player sees any hope of winning or when both players fear the risks they might incur by continuing to play.

Perpetual Check

Perpetual check comes about when a player can check endlessly without bringing the game to a decisive result. Where such a player suffers from a disadvantage in position or material or both, he is naturally satisfied to avoid losing by exploiting his power to maintain the checks indefinitely. His opponent is naturally reluctant to concede the draw, but if he cannot escape from the checks, then his hands are tied and the draw is unavoidable.

In Diagram 24 we have a good example of a perpetual check.

Diagram 24 (*White to play*)

BLACK

WHITE

Black is a Rook, Bishop, and Pawn ahead. This is a crushing advantage in material, and in the normal course of events White would be hopelessly lost.

However, White sees that he can save himself by giving perpetual check. He plays his Queen *diagonally* down to the last row, checking Black's King. Black's only reply is to play his King diagonally to the extreme file at the edge of the board. The resulting position is shown in Diagram 25.

White now plays his Queen back to its original position in Diagram 24, again giving check. In reply Black must move his King to its original square in the position of Diagram 24.

Now the position of Diagram 24 has been reached all over again. White repeats the check already shown, and Black must make the same reply, leading once more to the position of Diagram 25. And so the checks continue "perpetually"—Black is foiled, and the game must be called a draw.

Diagram 25 (*White to play*)

BLACK

WHITE

Inadequate Checkmating Material

There are certain basic positions in which checkmate can be forced with a minimum advantage in material (page 60). Where less than this basic minimum advantage is present, it will be impossible to force checkmate.

Thus, checkmate cannot be forced by a player who is left with the following reduced forces:

1. King and Bishop against King
2. King and Knight against King
3. King and two Knights against King

Stalemate

Stalemate, a form of drawn position, is so similar to checkmate that the resemblance confuses many players. Slight as the distinction is, it is of the utmost practical importance—for checkmate wins, whereas stalemate only draws.

Diagram 26 (*Black to play: Stalemate!*)

BLACK

WHITE

To understand the vital distinction, remember that *a King can never move into check.*

Checkmate (victory) results when a King *is in check* and there is no way to get the King out of check.

Stalemate (a draw) results when a player whose turn it is to move *is not in check* and is limited to moves that would put his King into check.

Diagram 26 illustrates this feature.

Black is *not* in check; it is his turn to move; he is limited to moves that would put his King into check.

This is *stalemate,* and despite Black's enormous disadvantage in material, the game is a draw.*

To many beginners it seems unjust that White, with his enormous advantage in material, should be penalized this way and deprived of victory. However, the stalemate idea is well grounded in the history of chess. Stalemate was originally introduced as a penalty for clumsy players who lacked the skill to turn a substantial material advantage into quick victory.

Draw by Repetition of Moves

Another method of bringing about a drawn game is by repetition of moves. (This is rarely seen in games between average players.)

If a position is about to be repeated a third time, with

---

* *If it were White's turn to move* in Diagram 26, he would have four different ways to force checkmate on the move. This highlights the difference between stalemate and checkmate.

the same player on the move each time, that player may rightfully claim a draw if he announces his intention of making the move that would bring about the threefold repetition.

The draw may also be claimed by a player who announces that the position has just been repeated three times, with the same player on the move each time.

This type of draw was doubtless conceived as a way of curbing players who make aimless moves and repeat the same moves because they cannot think of better ones. However, claiming the draw in this manner is almost unthinkable unless one can offer indisputable evidence that the threefold repetition is about to be completed or has been completed.

The best evidence is an accurate score of the game, with all the moves set down right after they were played. (The next chapter explains how moves are recorded.)

Fifty-Move Rule

When a player whose turn it is demonstrates that the past 50 (or more) moves have been made without a piece having been captured or a Pawn moved, he can claim a draw.

This type of claim, too, can hardly be maintained without recourse to an undisputed record of the game.

CHAPTER 2

How Chess Moves Are Recorded

CHESS notation serves a variety of useful purposes. It makes it possible to keep a permanent record of a game for future reference. Using this record, a player can go over a game in order to evaluate the play, determine which moves were good and which were bad, and examine the alternatives to what was actually played.

And, what is perhaps even more important, it becomes possible to study chess, improving one's playing strength and increasing one's enjoyment of the game by making use of the printed record of play.

The basic underlying ideas of chess notation are very simple. Obviously every chessman must have a name, and every square on the chessboard must have a name. Moves can then be recorded under the general formula, "Unit x moves from square m to square n."

Still a third element is needed: the exact order of moves must be known. For this purpose, the moves are numbered.

The opening position makes a useful beginning for naming the pieces and Pawns.

NAMING THE PIECES AND PAWNS

Diagram 27

BLACK

WHITE

The names and abbreviations of the White pieces, reading from left to right, are:

1. Queen Rook (QR)
2. Queen Knight (QN)
3. Queen Bishop (QB)
4. Queen (Q)
5. King (K)

6. King Bishop (KB)
7. King Knight (KN)
8. King Rook (KR)

Thus, the names of the three White pieces to the left of the White Queen are preceded by the word "Queen." The names of the three White pieces to the right of the White King are preceded by the word "King."

Still referring to the opening position in Diagram 27, each Pawn is named for the piece in front of which it is placed. The names and abbreviations of the White Pawns, reading from left to right, are:

1. Queen Rook Pawn (QRP)
2. Queen Knight Pawn (QNP)
3. Queen Bishop Pawn (QBP)
4. Queen Pawn (QP)
5. King Pawn (KP)
6. King Bishop Pawn (KBP)
7. King Knight Pawn (KNP)
8. King Rook Pawn (KRP)

The Black pieces and Pawns have the identical names as their White opposite numbers on the same files. Thus, White's Queen Rook and Queen Rook Pawn face Black's Queen Rook and Queen Rook Pawn along the same file.

THE NAMES OF THE SQUARES

Each file (vertical row) on the chessboard is named for the White and Black pieces which stand on it at the beginning of the game. Starting from White's extreme left and from Black's extreme right, the files are named as follows:

1. Queen Rook file
2. Queen Knight file
3. Queen Bishop file
4. Queen file
5. King file
6. King Bishop file
7. King Knight file
8. King Rook file

The names of the files are permanent, in order to provide a fixed frame of reference. Even when the pieces and Pawns have left their original squares—or disappeared altogether—the files keep their names.

However, a rank (horizontal row) has two names. One name is used for recording White's moves; the other name is used for recording Black's moves.

The rank on which White's pieces are placed at the beginning of the game is called "White's first rank." All the squares in this rank are "one"-squares. Thus, the square on which White's Queen Rook originally stands is always "Queen Rook one" (QR1) at any stage of the game, *as long as a White move is being described.*

The rank on which White's Pawns originally stand is "White's second rank." All these squares are "two"-squares for White moves. Thus, White's King Pawn (KP) originally stands on King two or King 2 (K2).

The rank in front of White's Pawns is "White's third rank," and all the squares in it are "three"-squares for all White moves. Thus, if White's King Pawn advances one square, the move is written "P–K3."

The remaining ranks, from White's point of view, are:

White's fourth rank ("four"-squares)
White's fifth rank ("five"-squares)
White's sixth rank ("six"-squares)
White's seventh rank ("seven"-squares)
White's eighth rank ("eight"-squares)

From Black's side of the board the squares are named in similar fashion. The rank on which pieces originally stand is "Black's first rank." (This is White's eighth rank.) In recording Black's moves, all squares on his first rank are "one"-squares. Thus, the square on which Black's King stands is King 1 (K1) for *Black* moves, and King 8 (K8) for *White* moves.

The rank on which Black's Pawns stand at the beginning of the game is *Black's* second rank ("two"-

squares) for *Black* moves—and White's seventh rank ("seven"-squares) for *White* moves. Thus, the square on which Black's King Pawn originally stands is King 2 (K2) for *Black* moves, and King 7 (K7) for *White* moves.

The rank on which White's Pawns stand at the beginning of the game is *Black's* seventh rank ("seven"-squares) for *Black* moves—and White's second rank ("two"-squares) for *White* moves.

Diagram 28

BLACK

QR1 / QR8	QN1 / QN8	QB1 / QB8	Q1 / Q8	K1 / K8	KB1 / KB8	KN1 / KN8	KR1 / KR8
QR2 / QR7	QN2 / QN7	QB2 / QB7	Q2 / Q7	K2 / K7	KB2 / KB7	KN2 / KN7	KR2 / KR7
QR3 / QR6	QN3 / QN6	QB3 / QB6	Q3 / Q6	K3 / K6	KB3 / KB6	KN3 / KN6	KR3 / KR6
QR4 / QR5	QN4 / QN5	QB4 / QB5	Q4 / Q5	K4 / K5	KB4 / KB5	KN4 / KN5	KR4 / KR5
QR5 / QR4	QN5 / QN4	QB5 / QB4	Q5 / Q4	K5 / K4	KB5 / KB4	KN5 / KN4	KR5 / KR4
QR6 / QR3	QN6 / QN3	QB6 / QB3	Q6 / Q3	K6 / K3	KB6 / KB3	KN6 / KN3	KR6 / KR3
QR7 / QR2	QN7 / QN2	QB7 / QB2	Q7 / Q2	K7 / K2	KB7 / KB2	KN7 / KN2	KR7 / KR2
QR8 / QR1	QN8 / QN1	QB8 / QB1	Q8 / Q1	K8 / K1	KB8 / KB1	KN8 / KN1	KR8 / KR1

WHITE

Diagram 28 shows how all the squares on the board are named.

Each square in Diagram 28 has a White name, with the corresponding Black name printed upside down on the same square. When a *White* move is made, the *White* name of the square is used. When a *Black* move is made, the *Black* name of the square is used.

HOW TO READ MOVES

The moves of a game are recorded in two columns—the first column for White's moves, the second column for Black's moves. To follow the right sequence of moves, play White's first move, then read across for Black's reply (his first move).

Sometimes the columns are broken up by notes on the moves. When a move is made that calls for a comment, the record of the moves is temporarily halted in order to explain the most recent move made, or to prepare the reader for what is coming, or to suggest an alternative to what has just been played.

Here is a sample sequence:

	WHITE	BLACK
1	P–K4	P–K4
2	N–KB3	N–QB3
3	B–N5	. . .

The resulting situation is shown in Diagram 29.

Diagram 29 *(Black to play)*

BLACK

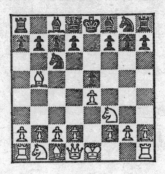

WHITE

The preceding moves are now explained one at a time:

WHITE   BLACK

1 P–K4   ...

White starts by advancing his King Pawn two squares. (When a note is written to a White move, it is necessary to omit Black's reply for the time being. Consequently, when the moves are resumed, the reader must look for *Black's* reply in the second column.)

1 ...   P–K4

This is Black's first move. He has advanced his King

Pawn two squares. White's second move will appear in the left column.

2 N–KB3   . . .

White has played his King Knight to King Bishop 3. (It is not necessary to write *KN* here—*N* is sufficient, as only one White Knight can go to his King Bishop 3.)

2 . . .   N–QB3

Black has played his Queen Knight to Queen Bishop 3.

3 B–N5   . . .

White has played his King Bishop to Queen Knight 5. (This is abbreviated to "B–N5" as only one Bishop can go to one Knight 5. If either Bishop could go to either Knight 5, the move would have to be described more precisely: B–QN5.)

With 3 B–N5 the position of Diagram 29 is reached.

When referring to a move in a note, many books (including this one) differentiate between White and Black moves in order to make the situation quite clear to the reader.

For example, the statement "P–K4 is a good move" may confuse a reader, who may ask himself, "Whose 1 P–K4? White's 1 P–K4? Black's 1 P–K4?"

To eliminate confusion, Black's moves are preceded

by leaders, thus: . . . P–K4. Consequently there is no confusion in such a sentence as: "1 P–K4 is a good move, and 1 . . . P–K4 is a good reply."

Sometimes a whole sequence of moves is run together in a single sentence. For example: "The opening moves we have just played over were 1 P–K4, P–K4; 2 N–KB3, N–QB3; 3 B–N5."

In this "running notation," White's moves are recorded first and follow the sequence number (1, 2, 3, etc.). Black's moves follow the comma and precede the semicolon.

Sometimes a sequence of moves in running notation starts with a Black move. In order to put the reader on his guard, the sequence begins with leaders. Example: "After 1 P–K4, the game continued 1 . . . P–K4; 2 N–KB3, N–QB3; 3 B–N5."

SYMBOLS USED IN NOTATION

So far the only notation symbols used have been the abbreviations for pieces, Pawns, and squares, and a dash indicating that a chess unit moves to a certain square. Here is a complete list of the symbols used in chess notation:

King	K
Queen	Q
Rook	R

Bishop   B
Knight   N
Pawn   P
captures   x
moves to —
check   ch
discovered check   dis ch
double check   dbl ch
en passant (in passing)   e.p.
castles King-side   o—o
   (not used in this book)
castles Queen-side   o—o—o
   (not used in this book)
a good move   !
a very good move   ! !
a bad move   ?
a very bad move   ? ?
from or at   /
promotes to a Queen   /Q

HOW TO AVOID AMBIGUITY

Sometimes a unit has the possibility of capturing two or three units of the same kind. It then becomes necessary to specify with utmost precision just which unit has been captured. An example of this occurs in Diagram 30.

White's next move is written, "NxP/B3." Wouldn't it have been sufficient to write "NxP"? No, for the

Diagram 30 (*White to play*)

BLACK

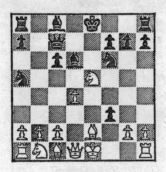

WHITE

White Knight at King 5 can capture any one of three Black Pawns. Even writing "NxBP" would be inadequate, for the Knight has a choice of capturing the Black Queen Bishop Pawn or either of Black's King Bishops Pawns. In fact, even "NxKBP" would not be good enough, for there are two Black King Bishop Pawns which can be captured.

However, "NxP/B3" conveys the meaning perfectly. This is shorthand for: "White's Knight at King 5 captures the Black Pawn at White's King Bishop 3 square."

Another type of ambiguity arises when two like pieces of the same color can go to the same square. This calls for some way of making it clear just which piece has moved. Diagram 31 is a case in point.

Diagram 31 (*Black to play*)

BLACK

WHITE

Black plays one of his Knights to King 5. To write, ". . . N–K5" is not enough, as it does not tell *which* Black Knight goes to King 5. Suppose it is the Black Knight on Q3 that makes the move. Then the move is written ". . . N/Q3–K5." And if the other Black Knight moves, this is recorded as ". . . N/B3–K5." In this way there can be no doubt as to which Black Knight has moved.

The survey of the rules and fundamentals of chess has now been completed. The remaining chapters deal with the mechanics of winning, and the ways in which a winning position may be built up.

CHAPTER 3

Winning Methods

IN chess there are certain types of checkmate positions that can be forced when a great deal of material has been captured and removed from the board. What makes these checkmates possible is that one of the players is considerably ahead in material.

This chapter will deal with the three elements that powerfully influence the course of a game:

1. *The basic checkmates*
2. *The relative value of the forces*
3. *Ways of winning material*

THE BASIC CHECKMATES

When a player is ahead in material, he can play to exchange forces repeatedly, coming down to a greatly simplified position in which he can force one of the basic checkmates. Thus, a knowledge of these basic situations gives him a positive goal to aim for. With this knowledge as a foundation, he can enrich and broaden his ability to win games.

Checkmate can be forced in any of these simplified situations:

1. King and Queen against a lone King.
2. King and Rook against a lone King.
3. King and two Bishops against a lone King.
4. King, Bishop, and Knight against a lone King.

CHECKMATE BY THE QUEEN

To bring about this checkmate, it is necessary to confine the lone King to one of the four side rows of the

Diagram 32 (*Black is checkmated*)

BLACK

WHITE

board, with the stronger side's King cutting off the escape of the opponent's King. The typical final position is shown in Diagram 32. (For a description of the actual process of forcing checkmate with the Queen, *see* pages 133–134.)

In the position of Diagram 32, Black's King, which is in check, has no way of getting out of check. White has won the game. (For an alternative checkmate position with the Queen, see Diagram 64.)

CHECKMATE BY THE ROOK

This checkmate too can only be brought about by confining the lone King to one of the four side rows of the board, with the stronger side's King cutting off escape of the lone King. The typical final position is shown in Diagram 33. (For a description of the actual process of forcing checkmate with Rook, *see* pages 135–136.)

Diagram 33 (*White is checkmated*)

BLACK

WHITE

In the position of Diagram 33, White's King, which is in check, has no way of getting out of check. Black has won the game.

CHECKMATE BY THE TWO BISHOPS

This checkmate can only be brought about by confining the lone King to one of the corner squares, with the stronger side's King nearby to cut off any attempt to escape. The typical final position is shown in Diagram 34. (The actual checkmating process is given on pages 137–138.)

Diagram 34 (*Black is checkmated*)

BLACK

WHITE

In the position of Diagram 34, Black's King, which is in check, has no way of getting out of check. White has won the game.

Diagram 35 (*White is checkmated*)

BLACK

WHITE

CHECKMATE BY BISHOP AND KNIGHT

This checkmate can only be brought about by confining the lone King to a corner square of the same color as those the Bishop travels on. The typical final position is shown in Diagram 35. (The actual checkmating process is given on pages 139–141.)

In the position of Diagram 35, White's King, which is in check, has no way of getting out of check. Black has won the game.

MATERIAL ADVANTAGE

A material advantage comes about through a series of moves in which a player captures a hostile man and loses one of his own of lesser value (*see* page 67). For example, White allows a Pawn to be captured in exchange for his capturing a Black Knight.

The prime reason why material advantage is important is that in many cases it leads to the basic checkmate positions just shown. By constantly forcing exchanges, a player with a material advantage can reduce the position to one where a basic checkmate becomes feasible.

In practice what often happens is that the opponent, foreseeing what is bound to happen as a result of his material disadvantage, resigns the game; he concedes that checkmate is inevitable.

It is true (as pointed out on pages 43–44) that certain types of material advantage cannot force checkmate. For example, King and Knight cannot checkmate a lone King.

However, if there are still *other forces on the board*, the stronger side is sure to win. Superior force makes the attack stronger than the defense. The weaker side, being outnumbered, must succumb. This is well brought out in the play from Diagram 37, in which the advantage of a Knight ahead makes the weaker side's resistance hopeless.

HOW MATERIAL ADVANTAGE IS CREATED

Since material advantage almost invariably leads to victory, it is useful to know the ways in which it is most often acquired.

1. Threats to win material achieve their objective when the opponent overlooks the threat or defends inefficiently.

2. A player gives check and simultaneously attacks another hostile unit.

3. A player simultaneously attacks two or more hostile units.

4. Standard attacking methods, such as the "pin" and the "fork" (described in Chapter 5), often win material.

RELATIVE VALUE OF THE FORCES

Opportunities for exchanging (capturing a hostile unit in return for a friendly unit) arise constantly in the course of a game. If a player is not absolutely clear about the comparative value of these units, he doesn't know whether to go into a given exchange or to avoid it; he must spend a lot of time wondering about a matter which is—or should be—routine knowledge.

In this section the relative value of all the chess units is explained. (Only the King is omitted, as this piece cannot be exchanged.) Having this information will make a player more confident and add considerably to his powers of calculation, planning, and judgment of position.

Long experience has made it possible to assign the following values to the chess forces:

Queen   9 points
Rook   5 points
Bishop   3 points
Knight   3 points
Pawn   1 point

These values hold good in the overwhelming majority of instances. By taking them into account, a player will be guided in making up his mind about exchanging possibilities. He will also have a clear notion about what is involved when he wins or loses material.

For example, the table indicates that Bishop and Knight are of equal value, and one may be freely exchanged for the other.

A Rook and two Pawns (7 points) are more valuable than a Bishop and Knight (6 points).

A player who gives up his Queen (9 points) for his opponent's two Rooks (10 points) will generally obtain the advantage. This is important information, for most players are reluctant to part with the Queen, even when this involves a favorable transaction.

A player who loses his Queen (9 points) for a Rook (5 points) or for a Bishop or Knight (3 points) is sure to lose. He will be helpless against the far-ranging Queen.

When a player has a Rook (5 points) against a Bishop or Knight (3 points), he is said to be "the Exchange ahead," or to have "won the Exchange." If he has a Bishop or Knight against a Rook, he is said to be "the Exchange down," or to have "lost the Exchange."

Inexperienced players will readily give up a Bishop or Knight (3 points) for a mere Pawn (1 point) and have nothing to show for this transaction. If such players were familiar with the table of relative value, they would avoid these losing captures. Diagram 36 illustrates this possibility.

For White to play NxP? here would be all wrong, as Black simply replies . . . NxN, having won a piece for a Pawn.

On the other hand, in the position of Diagram 36 it would be perfectly unobjectionable for White to play BxN. For, after Black replies . . . QPxB or . . .

Diagram 36 (*White to play*)

BLACK

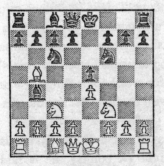

WHITE

NPxB, White has captured a Knight and Black has captured a Bishop. According to the table of relative value, this is a perfectly even exchange, so that both sides can be content with the transaction.

SUPERIOR FORCE MUST TELL

Superior force, aside from occasional positions, will always lead to new advantages: decisive threats, decisive attacks, new gains of material, checkmate possibilities. In many cases the opponent, overwhelmed by the sheer weight of the extra material against him, will resign the unequal struggle.

This is convincingly demonstrated in Diagram 37.

If there were no Pawns on the board, Black's advantage of a Knight would be useless, as he could not

Diagram 37 (*Black to play*)

BLACK

WHITE

force checkmate (page 44). But the presence of the Pawn changes the whole picture. White's unassisted King cannot be everywhere. Sooner or later, the agile Knight will win Pawns which White is powerless to defend. Black can convert his Pawn advantage into a new Queen (pages 141–144), thereby acquiring the material advantage which will make it possible for him to force checkmate.

In the position of Diagram 37, play proceeds:

WHITE   BLACK
1   . . .   N–N5ch!

A typical situation. The Knight gives check and simultaneously attacks White's King Rook Pawn. White must move his King out of check, whereupon Black continues . . . NxP, increasing his material advantage. Further material gains by Black are inevitable, thanks to the agile leaps of his Knight. Eventually he will win along the lines laid down in the previous comment.

SIMPLIFYING EXCHANGES FORCE THE ISSUE

Once a player has a material advantage, endless opportunities for simplifying exchanges will present themselves. These exchanges favor the stronger side for a variety of reasons:

1. They hasten the time when he will be able to checkmate in one of the basic checkmating situations.

2. They reduce the possibility of complications which offer his opponent the only chance of "swindling" his way out of trouble.

3. Finally, they generally lead to gaining of additional material. This is illustrated in Diagram 38.

Diagram 38 (*White to play*).

BLACK

WHITE

White is a Rook ahead, and with this huge material advantage he can win as he pleases. (At all times there is a latent threat of a ruthless series of exchanges that will reduce the situation to White King and Rook against the lone Black King—a basic checkmating position.)

WHITE	BLACK
1 R–Q8ch!	...

A simplifying exchange to force the disappearance of Black's remaining Rook.

1 ...   RxR

Black of course has no choice.

2 RxRch   K–B2
3 R–Q7ch   ...

White has achieved his major objective (exchange of Rooks). But he will also win a Pawn. And in addition the remaining material is too reduced for Black to be able to create any complications.

WHEN SUPERIOR FORCE DOESN'T WIN

As a general proposition, superior force must tell; but this does not take into account the possibility that a player may blunder and thus deprive himself of the victory to which he is theoretically entitled. Diagram 39 illustrates such a situation.

White has two Rooks against Rook and Knight: he has won the Exchange, and his superiority in force should win the game. To demonstrate this, he relies on the fact his two Rooks are more powerful—that is, have more mobility and hence more striking power—than Black's Rook and Knight.

WHITE   BLACK
1 R–Q1!   ...

Diagram 39 (*White to play*)

BLACK

WHITE

Well played. This is a double attack on the Black Knight, which cannot move away, for then the Black Rook would be lost. (This is a "pin," explained on pages 121–125). Thus White wins the Knight, which is attacked twice and defended only once. White thereby increases his material advantage to an overwhelming extent.

1 ...   R–QB1!?

Black desperately sets a trap. If White now plays 2R/K5xN! he has an easy win based on his enormous material advantage.

2 R/Q1xN?? ...

Fatal overconfidence. White falls into a deadly trap and loses the game despite his apparently crushing material advantage.

2	. . .	R–B8ch
3	R–Q1	RxRch
4	R–K1	RxR mate

White's King is in check, and cannot escape from check. Thus White is checkmated. There is a valuable moral here: material advantage should generally enable a player to checkmate his opponent, but a blunder can transform the picture. *The safety of one's King overrules every other consideration.*

SACRIFICING MATERIAL

There is one type of position in which a player may knowingly disregard the table of relative values. On such occasions he can give up material—sometimes considerable material—in order to obtain more than adequate compensation. Thus, a player may give up his Queen—"sacrifice" it—in order to bring about checkmate. But such moves must be calculated with the most rigorous accuracy.

CHAPTER 4

Guide to Opening Play

THE opening—the beginning stage—is that part of the game in which the players bring their pieces into action and try to build up a favorable formation for the ensuing play.

The knowledge of a few broad general principles can make all the difference between getting a playable position or one which is so wretched that it offers no prospects for constructive planning.

BASIC RULES FOR OPENING PLAY

1. Always start (with White) by advancing a center pawn two squares; 1 P–K4 is strongly recommended.
2. Develop pieces rapidly and effectively.
3. Avoid losing time.
4. Avoid self-limiting moves.
5. Don't neglect the safety of the King.

ALWAYS START BY ADVANCING A CENTER PAWN

There are two chief reasons for White's starting the game with 1 P–K4, and for Black's replying with 1 . . . P–K4.

1. 1 P–K4 opens lines for the King Bishop and the Queen. (The early move with this Bishop is one of the necessary preliminaries to castling.)

2. Center Pawns advanced to the fourth rank prevent hostile pieces from occupying the valuable center squares controlled by those Pawns. This is of the greatest importance, for experience shows that Knights and Bishops are posted most effectively on the center squares or near the center squares.

These recommendations would have helped Black to avoid the following very bad opening moves:

WHITE	BLACK
1 P–K4	P–KB3?

Here 1 . . . P–K4 was the move.

2	P–Q4	P–K3
3	N–KB3	P–Q3
4	N–B3	P–B3
5	B–Q3	P–KN3
6	B–KB4	P–N3
7	Castles	B–KN2

The resulting position appears in Diagram 40.

The "hedgehog" type of opening play Black has adopted here is seen very often. At a loss how to proceed, he helplessly makes one timid move after another.

Diagram 40 (*White to play*)

BLACK

WHITE

White, on the other hand, purposefully plays out his King Pawn and Queen Pawn two squares.

The result: White's center Pawns control the center squares King 5 and Queen 5; no Black pieces can be posted on those valuable squares. Furthermore, White's Knights control these squares, and for good measure White's Bishop on King Bishop 4 also controls King 5.

This opening sequence has many other instructive features which are brought out in the following discussion.

DEVELOP PIECES EFFECTIVELY AND EFFICIENTLY

Bringing out the pieces rapidly and effectively makes both attack and efficient defense against the opponent's threats possible.

On the other hand, if a player lets his pieces roost on their home squares, they will not menace the opponent's position. Such a player cannot make plans, because he has nothing to work with; and he is likely to be helpless against the opponent's threats.

In the situation of Diagram 40, for example, White has developed both Knights, both Bishops, and castled. (This last counts as a developing move, as White has transferred his King to a safe place.)

Black, on the other hand, has developed only one piece, his King Bishop. Even this piece has no scope because it is blocked by Black's King Bishop Pawn.

Even an inexperienced player can see that White's position, with so many pieces in *active* play, is full of potential energy and lively possibilities. Black's position, on the other hand, is cramped and absolutely without constructive prospects.

The following example drastically demonstrates how quickly neglected development of the pieces can lead to disaster. White makes the following mistakes:

1. He wastes time by moving Pawns instead of pieces.

2. He plays out a Bishop before either Knight.

3. He makes no preparation for castling, thereby creating potential danger for his King.

WHITE	BLACK
1 P–Q4	. . .

As previously recommended, 1 P–K4 is safer and creates less difficulty for the average player.

1 ... N–KB3

While it is true that 1 ... P–Q4 is safer, Black's Knight move has points because it is a *developing* move. Besides, the Knight move helps control the center.

2 P–QB4 ...

Another Pawn move. It controls the Queen 5 square, to be sure, but White should be thinking about developing his pieces.

2 ... P–K4

An attempt to confuse White—and it works!

White should now continue with 3 PxP, N–N5; 4 B–B4, N–QB3; 5 N–KB3, still defending his extra Pawn while he concentrates on steady development. Even if Black later recovers his Pawn by making ... N/N5xKP possible, it will be at the cost of moving this Knight three times in the opening—a loss of time which involves neglected development of his pieces.

3 P–Q5? ...

This loses time. Worse yet, it neglects the development of the White pieces.

3 ... B–B4!

Black immediately profits by White's last move to develop the Bishop effectively. With three moves made on each side, Black has developed two pieces, White has developed none. Clearly White has mismanaged the opening.

4 B–N5? ...

At last a developing move, but a very ill-judged one. The right move was 4 N–KB3, and the reasons for this are widely applicable.

In the first place, it is advisable to develop at least one Knight before developing a Bishop. The Knights are short-stepping pieces. Almost invariably the King Bishop 3 square is the best spot for the King Knight; the Queen Bishop 3 square is the best spot for the

Diagram 41 *(Black to play)*

BLACK

WHITE

Queen Knight. However, it is not always so clear where a Bishop should play, as this is a far-ranging piece with a choice of several moves. Hence, "Knights before Bishops" is a sound principle.

Second, it is generally advisable to play out the King-side pieces first, in order to give the King more protection and in order to set the stage for castling. Here White has violated both principles.

4 . . .   N–K5 ! !

Black "sacrifices" his Queen (*see* page 74) and for a very good reason.

5 BxQ   BxP mate

White's opening play had to be very bad to result in checkmate after only five moves.

AVOID LOSING TIME

Losing time in the opening may be the result of one or more of these mistaken policies:

1. Making too many Pawn moves.
2. Moving the same piece repeatedly.
3. Devoting a great deal of effort to some comparatively unimportant material gain.
4. Developing the Queen prematurely.

Inexperienced players are so fascinated by the Queen's enormous power that they tend to develop this all-important piece much too soon. The result, as a rule, is that the Queen is harried by the attack of hostile units of lesser value.

An example:

WHITE	BLACK
1 P–K4	P–K4
2 P–Q4	. . .

Premature (2N–KB3 is better).

| 2 . . . | PxP |
| 3 QxP | N–QB3! |

Black develops his Queen Knight—a good move in itself, and doubly good here *because it gains time by attacking the White Queen.* See Diagram 42.

Diagram 42 (*White to play*)

BLACK

WHITE

AVOID SELF-LIMITING MOVES

On principle, it is weakening and in some cases even dangerous to play moves that reduce the mobility of your own forces. Here is a case in point:

WHITE	BLACK
1 P–K4	P–K4
2 P–Q3?	...

White's 2 P–Q3? was a mistake because it *closed the diagonal of his King Bishop before that piece had a chance to develop aggressively.* Thus, with a future B–QB4 or B–QN5 ruled out, the Bishop is condemned to a rather useless existence inside the wall of the White Pawns.

Diagram 43 (*Black to play*)

BLACK

WHITE

Black, on the other hand, has not moved his Queen
Pawn and is therefore able to develop his King Bishop
efficiently.

Another type of self-limiting move which is frequently encountered appears in the play arising from
Diagram 44.

Diagram 44 (*White to play*)

BLACK

WHITE

In general, you must be cautious about advancing
Pawns in the opening. While the Pawn move may seem
of trifling importance, the consequences may be grave
indeed. That is the case in Diagram 44.

White's Bishop at Queen Knight 5 is attacked. His
only correct course is 1 BxBch, which Black answers
with 1 . . . NxB—an even exchange. Instead, White
blunders:

WHITE	BLACK
1 B–B4?	P–QN4!
2 B–N3	. . .

2 B–Q3 is answered in the same way, with the same result.

2 . . .	P–B5!

Winning a piece, as the attacked Bishop is trapped. White was at fault in failing to foresee that his Bishop would have no escape. *Avoid self-limiting moves.*

GUARD THE KING

Most players become so preoccupied with other matters that they completely ignore the safety of their King. The usual consequence is that they forget to castle into comparative safety. Instead, they leave the King on its original square, where it often becomes exposed to attack.

In some cases the center lines are opened, giving the opponent quick access to the vulnerable King's headquarters. In other cases a player gets himself involved prematurely in all sorts of projects, instead of attending to his King's safety.

Two brief, drastic examples show what is likely to happen when the King's safety is ignored.

	WHITE	BLACK
1	P–K4	P–K4
2	P–KB4	PxP

See pages 92–93 regarding these moves.

	WHITE	BLACK
3	N–KB3	P–KN4
4	B–B4	. . .

Danger signal for Black: White already has two pieces developed, whereas Black has none. Consequently, development with 4 . . . B–N2 is safe and good.

4 . . .   P–KB3??

Diagram 45 (*White to play*)

BLACK

WHITE

Black's last move is a blunder that allows White to "sacrifice" a Knight with crushing effect.

5 NxP!   PxN
6 Q–R5ch   . . .

This powerful invasion forced quick checkmate.

6 . . .   K–K2
7 Q–B7ch   K–Q3
8 Q–Q5ch   K–K2
9 Q–K5 mate

Equally mistaken is the thoughtless policy of embarking on extended maneuvers and thereby neglecting the King's welfare:

WHITE	BLACK
1 P–K4	P–QB3
2 P–Q4	P–Q4
3 N–QB3	PxP
4 NxP	N–B3
5 Q–Q3	P–K4
6 PxP	Q–R4ch
7 B–Q2	QxKP

Black threatens to win White's Knight on the King 4 square. Instead of guarding this piece, White plays an amazingly deep reply.

8 Castles!   NxN? ?

Black sees that on 8 . . . QxN White has 9 R–K1, pinning and winning Black's Queen. (The power of pins is explained on pages 121–125.) But the apparently profitable alternative that Black has selected is even worse.

9   Q–Q8ch! !   KxQ
10   B–KN5dbl ch   . . .

Diagram 46 (*White to play*)

BLACK

WHITE

A double check (*see* pages 39–40).

10   . . .   K–B2

If 10 . . . K–K1; 11 R–Q8 mate.

11   B–Q8 mate

White took brilliant advantage of Black's crass neglect of his King's safety.

THE CHIEF OPENINGS

There are many approved ways of starting a game. Many of these methods involve a specific sequence of moves for both players. Each of these standard sequences is identified by name.

To beginners, this multiplicity of "openings" is bewildering. Actually, the openings can be grouped in a number of easily understood classifications:

1. Double King Pawn openings: White plays 1 P–K4 and Black replies 1 . . . P–K4.
2. Single King Pawn openings: White plays 1 P–K4 and Black chooses a reply other than 1 . . . P–K4.
3. Double Queen Pawn openings: White plays 1 P–Q4 and Black replies 1 . . . P–Q4.
4. Single Queen Pawn openings: White plays 1 P–Q4 and Black chooses a reply other than 1 . . . P–Q4.

In the following pages the most important openings are listed alphabetically under their special groupings. In each case the moves which characterize an opening are given, and its basic character is briefly explained.

DOUBLE KING PAWN OPENINGS

Center Game

1	P–K4	P–K4
2	P–Q4	PxP
3	QxP	. . .

As explained earlier (*see* page 81), this is not a good opening for White. By developing his Queen prematurely, he allows Black to gain time with 3 . . . N–QB3.

Danish Gambit

	WHITE	BLACK
1	P–K4	P–K4
2	P–Q4	PxP
3	P–QB3	. . .

This is a "gambit"—from an Italian word which means to "trip up." A gambit is an opening in which a player offers material speculatively in order to get a big lead in development or some other advantage.

Here White intends to answer 3 . . . PxP with 4 B–QB4 and if 4 . . . PxP; 5 QBxP. In return for the two sacrificed Pawns, White has a powerful development which *may* give him a strong attack if Black does not bend all his efforts to catching up in development.

Evans Gambit

WHITE	BLACK
1 P–K4	P–K4
2 N–KB3	N–QB3
3 B–B4	B–B4
4 P–QN4	. . .

An offshoot of the Giuoco Piano (*see below*). White's idea is that on 4 . . . BxNP he will play 5 P–B3, followed by P–Q4 with a strong Pawn center and quick development with excellent attacking potential. Some of the most dashing examples of brilliant attacking play have developed from this opening. The prudent course for an inexperienced player is 4 . . . B–N3 (declining the gambit). This leads to a safe and uneventful game.

Four Knights' Game

WHITE	BLACK
1 P–K4	P–K4
2 N–KB3	N–QB3
3 N–B3	N–B3

(Note that the same position may be reached by 2 N–KB3, N–KB3; 3 N–B3, N–B3—or 2 N–QB3, N–KB3; 3 N–B3, N–B3—or 2 N–QB3, N–QB3; 3 N–B3, N–B3.)

This opening is safe and not very lively, leading to even positions in which nothing very exciting is likely to happen. It is therefore a good opening for inexperienced players to adopt.

Giuoco Piano

WHITE	BLACK
1 P–K4	P–K4
2 N–KB3	N–QB3
3 B–B4	B–B4

This opening has a split personality. When White continues with P–Q3 and N–B3, the game takes a placid course. But if White plays 4 P–B3 with a view to 5 P–Q4, the play is tricky and abounds in pitfalls for Black.

King's Gambit

WHITE	BLACK
1 P–K4	P–K4
2 P–KB4	PxP

White gives up a Pawn in order to get a strong Pawn center (eventual P–Q4), hoping for a quick development and strong attacking chances. The resulting play is usually brisk and complicated. Black can play safe by declining the gambit with 2 . . . B–B4 (when 3 PxP? ? is a bad blunder because of 3 . . . Q–R5ch). Another way to decline the gambit is 2 . . . P–Q4

(Falkbeer Counter Gambit), but this is much more complicated than 2 . . . B–B4.

Petroff's Defense

WHITE	BLACK
1 P–K4	P–K4
2 N–KB3	N–KB3

Instead of defending his King Pawn, Black undertakes an immediate counterattack. This is a good line of play for those who are familiar with its finesses. For example, after 3 NxP, Black must not reply 3 . . . NxP? ? (for then 4 Q–K2! wins *). Instead, 3 . . . P–Q3!; 4 N–KB3, is then the proper course.

Philidor's Defense

WHITE	BLACK
1 P–K4	P–K4
2 N–KB3	P–Q3

The defense with the Queen Pawn (instead of the recommended 2 . . . N–QB3) is too passive and leaves Black with a crowded, cramped development.

Ruy Lopez

WHITE	BLACK
1 P–K4	P–K4
2 N–KB3	N–QB3
3 B–N5	. . .

---

* If then 4 . . . N–KB3?; 5 N–B6 dis ch wins Black's Queen.

Of all the Double King Pawn openings, this is the one most frequently adopted, as it gives White lasting pressure on Black's game. Black has many opportunities to go wrong.

Note, however, that at this point White is not yet threatening to win Black's King Pawn. Thus, if 3 . . . P–QR3 White does not win a Pawn by 4 BxN, QPxB; 5 NxP, as Black can recover the Pawn satisfactorily with 5 . . . Q–Q5! (or even 5 . . . Q–N4!). This is one of the few cases in which early Queen development is not disadvantageous.

Scotch Game

WHITE	BLACK
1 P–K4	P–K4
2 N–KB3	N–QB3
3 P–Q4	PxP
4 NxP	. . .

As White has lost time by moving his King Knight twice, Black has an easy game. He develops satisfactorily with 4 . . . N–B3 or 4 . . . B–B4.

Two Knights' Defense

WHITE	BLACK
1 P–K4	P–K4
2 N–KB3	N–QB3
3 B–B4	N–B3

Black's third move is occasionally played to avoid

the Giuoco Piano (*see* page 92). The result is a complicated game, especially if White plays 4 N–N5 with double attack on Black's King Bishop Pawn. Then, after 4 . . . P–Q4; 5 PxP, inexperienced players do well to avoid 5 . . . NxP; 6 NxBP!? (the famous Fried Liver Attack), KxN; 7 Q–B3ch, K–K3; 8 N–B3, in which it is easy for Black to go astray.

Best for Black is 5 . . . N–QR4 with interesting and difficult play.

Vienna Game

WHITE	BLACK
1 P–K4	P–K4
2 N–QB3	. . .

This opening is somewhat lacking in bite, as 2 N–QB3 puts less pressure on Black's game than 2 N–KB3.

SINGLE KING PAWN OPENINGS

These openings are harder to play—for either side—than the Double King Pawn openings. However, the Single King Pawn lines have the advantage for Black in that by avoiding 1 . . . P–K4 he prevents White from playing some favorite opening in which he may have some nasty tricks up his sleeve.

Alekhine's Defense

WHITE	BLACK
1 P–K4	N–KB3

The idea of this queer-looking move is to tempt
White to a wholesale Pawn advance (for example, 2
P–K5, N–Q4; 3 P–QB4, N–N3; 4 P–Q4, P–Q3; 4
P–B4. If White plays well, Black is apt to be left with
a difficult and crowded position. On the other hand,
resourceful play by Black may demonstrate that the
advanced White Pawns are weak and hard to maintain.
This is a good defense to play against a weaker opponent.

Caro-Kann Defense

WHITE	BLACK
1 P–K4	P–QB3

The usual follow-up is 2 P–Q4, with Black replying
2 . . . P–Q4. Thus Black disputes control of the center without committing himself to any of the "open"
games that result when both players advance their King
Pawns. The Caro-Kann is safe, stodgy, and respect-
able. Play it against formidable opponents.

Center Counter Game

WHITE	BLACK
1 P–K4	P–Q4

This defense is not recommended for Black. As a
rule the continuation is 2 PxP, QxP; 3 N–QB3 and
White gains time driving off Black's Queen which has
been brought out prematurely. (*See* Diagram 42.)

French Defense

WHITE	BLACK
1 P–K4	P–K3

As in the Caro-Kann, White continues 2 P–Q4 and
Black replies 2 . . . P–Q4, struggling for control of
the center.

This is a fine, fighting, solid defense, more risky than
the Caro-Kann but also more promising. Black may
often find his game somewhat constricted, but if he
is willing to plunge into complications, he may find
himself winning many a game because White is likely
to overextend himself. It is in the nature of this plucky
defense that Black's resources are often sturdier than
they seem to be at first sight.

Sicilian Defense

WHITE	BLACK
1 P–K4	P–QB4

The most promising and enterprising of all the non–
1 . . . P–K4 defenses. This is the ideal defense for a
player who wants an all-out struggle. It has the virtue
of preventing a powerful White Pawn-center by P–Q4
and it gives Black the choice of a variety of possible
plans for development.

DOUBLE QUEEN PAWN OPENINGS

These openings lead to an intricate type of maneuvering which often flares up unexpectedly in brilliant pyrotechnical displays. Judging the possibilities in these openings requires considerable experience and nicety of judgment. For this reason, it is a good idea for a player to steer clear of the Queen Pawn openings until he has graduated from the beginner class.

Queen's Gambit Accepted

WHITE	BLACK
1 P–Q4	P–Q4
2 P–QB4	PxP

This is not a real gambit, as White can recover the Pawn at will (for example, by 3 Q–R4ch).

Whether Black should make the capture with his Queen Pawn is debatable, as doing so destroys his Pawn control of the center. Although some great masters have shown great fondness for this defense, it is generally conceded that White gets a free hand in the center and consequently greater mobility for his pieces.

Queen's Gambit Declined

WHITE	BLACK
1 P–Q4	P–Q4
2 P–QB4	P–K3

(or 2 . . . P–QB3)

This opening gets its name from the fact that Black avoids capturing White's Queen Bishop Pawn—at least for the time being. Instead of capturing, Black supports his Queen Pawn with his King Pawn or Queen Bishop Pawn. Black's idea, at least in the opening stage, is to maintain a Pawn at his Queen 4 and thus dispute control of the center.

Both sides need to have considerable skill and knowledge to play this opening well. Generally White has much more mobility at the start than Black. White's Queen Bishop usually plays aggressively to King Knight 5; his other Bishop is likewise developed aggressively to Queen 3; and in many cases his King Knight takes a commanding post at King 5.

Black may often find himself in a steadily progressing squeeze unless he recognizes the emergency and takes steps to free himself. His prime difficulty is the development of his Queen Bishop, which is apt to be hemmed in by the Black Pawns on white squares (for example, the Black Pawns at Queen 4, Queen Bishop 3, and King 3). As this problem frequently recurs, it is useful to examine the Pawn "skeleton" of Black's common position in this opening, as shown in Diagram 47.

Black's Queen Bishop's dilemma in this situation is obvious enough. This piece is imprisoned behind the wall of Black Pawns. It will be necessary for Black to aim for the liberating moves . . . P–K4 or . . . P–QB4 in order to free himself.

Diagram 47

BLACK

WHITE

All in all, this is one of the most interesting openings in the whole chess repertoire. But it is wise not to attempt it until one has made a fair amount of progress as a chess player.

SINGLE QUEEN PAWN OPENINGS

As indicated in the foregoing discussion, Black's game is far from easy after he answers 1 P–Q4 with . . . P–Q4. For this reason, many players prefer to answer 1 P–Q4 with some other move—generally 1 . . . N–KB3. This move (or 1 . . . P–KB4) has the virtue of controlling White's King 4 square, thus fighting for control of the center.

But these alternative moves also have two psychological advantages. In the first place, they prevent White from playing the opening he intended to play. In the second place, they give Black some choice in selecting the kind of game *he* would like to play. This freedom is naturally good for Black's morale, as it relieves him of the depressing feeling of playing second fiddle to White.

Budapest Defense

WHITE	BLACK
1 P–Q4	N–KB3
2 P–QB4	P–K4

A speculative offer of a Pawn. After 3 PxP Black replies 3 . . . N–N5, intending . . . NxKP. White's best course is to continue quietly with his development, not bothering to protect the advanced Pawn and calmly going about his business while Black moves his King Knight three times. On the other hand, should White try to guard this Pawn, he will often get into difficulties (for example, after 4 P–B4? when Black can advantageously reply 4 . . . B–B4). *See also* page 79 for an example of time-wasting play by White in this opening.

Dutch Defense

WHITE	BLACK
1 P–Q4	P–KB4

(This is also seen in the sequence 1 P–Q4, P–K3; 2 P–QB4, P–KB4; although here White has the option of transposing into the French Defense with 2 P–K4.)

The Dutch Defense is a good line of play for aggressive players, as it often gives Black attacking chances. It is also quite elastic, as Black has the choice of playing . . . P–K3 followed by . . . P–Q4; or . . . P–K3 followed by . . . P–Q3; or . . . P–Q3 followed by . . . P–K4.

Gruenfeld Defense

WHITE	BLACK
1 P–Q4	N–KB3
2 P–QB4	P–KN3
3 N–QB3	P–Q4

In this defense Black generally gives up control of the center with a view to exerting pressure with his "fianchettoed" King Bishop when it plays to King Knight 2. A typical continuation is 4 PxP, NxP; 5 P–K4, NxN; 6 PxN, P–QB4! followed by . . . B–N2. It is debatable whether the strength of Black's Bishop on the long diagonal outweighs the strength of White's impressive Pawn center.

King's Indian Defense

WHITE	BLACK
1 P–Q4	N–KB3
2 P–QB4	. . .

This is more customary than 2 N–KB3, which is also playable.

2 . . .   P–KN3

Black intends to fianchetto his King Bishop (. . . B–N2) in conjunction with . . . P–Q3 and . . . P–K4. A typical continuation is: 3 N–QB3, B–N2; 4 P–K4, P–Q3; 5 N–B3, QN–Q2; 6 B–K2, Castles; 7 Castles, P–K4.

Black may subsequently play . . . PxP in order to lengthen the scope of his Bishop on the long diagonal. White may foil this plan by playing 8 P–Q5 at once. Black's indicated strategy in that case would be to retreat his King Knight and aim for . . . P–KB4, opening the King Bishop file for his King Rook and giving his pieces more playing space.

In general, this is a complicated, fighting defense which gives Black a solid position and many resources.

Nimzoindian Defense

WHITE	BLACK
1 P–Q4	N–KB3
2 P–QB4	P–K3
3 N–QB3	B–N5

This defense is one of the most popular lines of play against 1 P–Q4. Black leaves his Queen Pawn temporarily unmoved, as he controls White's King 4 square by means of . . . N–KB3. Thus White's P–K4 is ruled out for the time being. (At this point, White's Queen Knight is "pinned"—so that P–K4? is simply met by . . . NxP, and White cannot retake.)

Later on, Black can play . . . P–Q3 followed by . . . P–B4 or . . . P–K4; or he may decide to play . . . P–Q4 after all. He has quite a few plans at his disposal.

But White has possibilities too. Most of them center around his playing P–QR3 and provoking Black to play . . . BxN. In that case, White's use of his two Bishops will often give him a lasting advantage.

Again, White may play P–K4 later on with great effect, obtaining an overwhelming position in the center and putting Black completely on the defensive. The counterpoint of White's and Black's intentions and plans leads to an extremely interesting struggle, with good chances for both players.

Queen's Indian Defense

WHITE	BLACK
1 P–Q4	N–KB3
2 P–QB4	P–K3
3 N–KB3	P–QN3

Black's last move proclaims that he intends to control the long diagonal with . . . B–N2. The usual procedure is 4 P–KN3; B–N2; 5 B–N2. White posts his King Bishop on the long diagonal to counteract the influence of Black's Bishop.

On the whole White has more freedom and better prospects. Generally speaking, this opening leads to a placid type of game, less complex than the King's Indian or Nimzoindian lines.

This completes the survey of the most popular openings and the theories underlying them. This bird's-eye view of the openings is by no means a substitute for careful study and long experience. At the same time, however, this introduction to the openings can help the reader avoid many of the discouragements and difficulties which plague most beginners.

CHAPTER 5

Winning Goals of Middle Game Play

FOR most players the middle game is the most enjoyable part of chess. The middle game starts right after the opening, say about the twelfth move. With quite a few pieces developed, the players are ready for action. What general rules should guide them?

There are several features of middle game play which can be applied to a great many situations. The player should strive to give the utmost mobility to his pieces and to make them co-operate harmoniously.

BASIC RULES FOR THE MIDDLE GAME

MOBILITY OF THE PIECES

Superior mobility is often the key to success in the middle game. Generally speaking, the degree of mobility will depend on how well the player develops the pieces in the opening.

Here are some ways to estimate mobility and its usefulness:

1. Rooks are effective on open lines.

2. When Bishops are on clear, uncluttered diagonals, their mobility can be exploited the most.

3. If Knights are well posted in the center or near it, they will give maximum service.

4. The King should be moved to a spot where it will be reasonably well protected and out of harm's way.

5. The Queen can exert enormous power if placed in the thick of the fight and poised for moves in several directions.

On the other hand, a player whose pieces have little mobility is headed for trouble. In such cases the literal or numerical value of his pieces may be deceptive. This is effectively brought out in the following examples.

In going over the play from the diagrams in this chapter, it is a good idea to play the moves over first without studying the notes. Once the broad picture becomes clear, the notes to each move should be studied carefully, to see how individual moves fit into the general plan. Note especially how alternative moves or explanations enrich one's understanding of the winning process.

The outstanding features of this position are as follows:

Diagram 48 (*Black to play*)

BLACK

WHITE

1. Material is even.

2. White seems to be threatening to win a Pawn by QxRP.

3. Black's Bishops have terrific scope, while White's Bishop and Knight have little mobility.

How does Black proceed? Should he passively defend the menaced Pawn with . . . R–R1 or can he proceed in some more aggressive fashion?

WHITE	BLACK
1 . . .	B–B4!

Attacking White's Rook, which, thanks to the power of the Black Bishops, has no worth-while move.

2	N–Q3	BxN
3	QxB	QxRP

Black's initial Bishop move has led directly to winning the Queen Rook Pawn. Now White's Queen Knight Pawn, deprived of its natural Pawn protection, becomes the target.

4 P–R3 . . .

Diagram 49 (*Black to play*)

BLACK

WHITE

4 . . . P–R5!

Black threatens to win another Pawn. White's Pawn is "pinned" (*see* pages 121–125) as the reply 5 PxP?? would cost him his Rook.

5 P–QN4   PxP

Here, too, White's reply is dictated to him, for if 6 BxP, B–B6! and Black wins:

I 7 QxB, QxRch and Black wins the Bishop too; or
II 7 BxB, QxRch; 8 QxQ, RxQch and Black wins easily with the Exchange ahead.

      6 RxP   RxR
      7 BxR   Q–N6!

The point is that after 8 QxQ, PxQ Black's Queen Knight Pawn threatens to advance and become a new Queen. Then, after 9 B–R3, P–N7; 10 BxNP, BxB Black has an easy win with a piece ahead. *(See also* pages 143–145 on the power of passed Pawns.)

      8 Q–Q2   P–R6!

White resigns. To stop the Queen Rook Pawn from queening, White must play 9 BxRP, allowing 9 . . . QxB when Black wins effortlessly with his piece to the good.

Summary—Black utilized his superior mobility to win a Pawn, and then established a winning advantage with his threat of queening.

In Diagram 50 also Black has a marked advantage in mobility based on these factors:

1. His Queen is aggressively placed, whereas White's Queen is still on its original square.

2. Both Black Rooks have open files.

3. One of Black's Knights is powerfully "centralized." The other Knight is about to achieve the same state.

4. White's Bishops are lifeless.

5. In some cases Black can menace the White King.

Diagram 50 *(Black to play)*

BLACK

WHITE

WHITE	BLACK
1 . . .	BxN !

If now 2 BxB, N–B6ch! forcing 3 BxN or 3 PxN and thereby winning White's Queen (3 . . . RxQ).

| 2 PxB | N–K5 ! |

Disregarding the attack on his other Knight. Now Black threatens 3 . . . NxB; 4 QxN, N–B6ch again winning White's Queen.

If now 3 K–R1, N/K5xB; 4 QxN, N–B6! threatening 5 . . . QxRP mate and also 5 . . . RxQ, White would have to stop the mate and would therefore lose his Queen.

3 PxN   RxQP

(*See* Diagram 51.)

Diagram 51 (*White to play*)

BLACK

WHITE

Black has temporarily "sacrificed" a piece (*see* page 74), but he must regain it. White's Bishop on Queen 2 is pinned, for if it moves, Black wins White's Queen

by . . . RxQ. (If White tries 4 B–KN5, Black replies
4 . . . NxB! with a winning game.)

4	Q–N3	NxB!
5	QxKPch	K–R1

If White moves his attacked Rook, he loses: 6 KR–
K1, QxBPch; 7 K–R1, R–K5!; 8 Q–Q6, RxB; 9 RxR,
Q–B8ch!! (not 9 . . . QxR??; 10 QxR mate); 10
RxQ, RxR mate.

6	P–N3	Q–K5!
7	QxQ	RxQ

Threatening 8 . . . RxB in addition to 8 . . . NxR.
If White tries 8 KR–K1, *Black doubles Rooks on the
King file* with 8 . . . KR–K1. This pins and wins the
attacked Bishop, which must not move.

8	B–Q3	R–Q5

Still attacking two White units.

9	B–B2	NxR

Black has won the Exchange, with easy victory in
sight.

Summary—Black's superior mobility opened up a
whole series of threats on White's undeveloped game.
Black's concentrated pressure resulted in winning the
Exchange.

HARMONIOUS CO-OPERATION OF THE PIECES

If the pieces have been efficiently developed in the opening, they can co-operate to achieve victory. The cumulative power of such pieces conjures up irresistible threats as if by magic.

Co-operation Creates Winning Threats

In the position of Diagram 52 Black has a winning combination of dire threats based on the harmonious co-operation of his pieces.

Diagram 52 (*Black to play*)

BLACK

WHITE

Black's advantage is based on these factors:

1. His Rooks have complete control of the open Queen file.

2. His Queen and Rooks are aggressively placed to take part in the coming invasion of White's position.

3. White's Rooks are split and cannot communicate with each other.

4. His Queen has virtually no mobility. (The attack on the Knight is merely temporary.)

5. White's Bishop, still on its original square, has no range.

WHITE	BLACK
1 . . .	Q–B7!

Guarding the Knight, and setting up two formidable threats:

I 2 . . . R–Q8; 3 Q–B2, RxRch; 4 QxR, R–Q8 pinning and winning White's Queen—or 4 KxR, R–Q8 ch; 5 Q–K1, RxQch; 6 KxR, Q–K7 mate.

II 2 . . . N–K7ch; 3 K–R1, R–Q8; 4 Q–B2, RxR ch; 5 QxR, R–Q8; pinning and winning White's Queen.

Note how Black's control of the Queen file culminates in his invasion at Queen 8.

White now tries to parry the threats. He cannot do it by 2 Q–B2, N–K7ch; 3 K–R1, R–Q8; when he is helpless against the coming 4 . . . RxRch; 5 QxR, R–Q8.

                    2 R–B2   Q–Q8!

Now White must salvage his menaced Queen.

If now 3 QxQ, RxQch; 4 R–B1, RxRch; 5 KxR, R–
Q8ch and Black wins the Bishop. (For more on this
type of "double attack," *see* pages 127–130.)

Or if 3 R–B1, N–K7ch; 4 K moves, NxB and Black
has won a piece.

                    3 Q–B1   . . .

Diagram 53 illustrates this point.

              Diagram 53 (*Black to play*)

                         BLACK

                         WHITE

                    3 . . .   N–K5!

Now Black's threat is 4 . . . NxR; 5 KxN, QxQch;

6 KxQ, R–Q8ch and Black wins the Bishop, remaining a whole Rook ahead.

In this position White resigns, because he sees that all the following replies are unsatisfactory:

I   4 R–B3, Q–B7! and the coming . . . R–Q8 will be murderous.

II   4 R–K2, QxR!; 5 QxQ, R–Q8ch; 6 Q–B1, RxQch; 7 KxR, R–Q8ch and again Black wins the Bishop, remaining a whole piece ahead.

III   4 QxQ, RxQch; 5 R–B1, RxRch; 6 KxR, R–Q8ch and again Black wins the Bishop with a whole piece ahead.

IV   4 R/R7–R2, NxR; 5 RxN, Q–N6!; 6 R–K2, R–Q8; 7 R–K1, RxR; 8 QxR, R–Q8 again pinning and winning the White Queen.

Summary—The harmonious co-operation of Black's pieces resulted in a crushing invasion along the Queen file. White was helpless against this invasion because his pieces were unable to work together properly.

In the position of Diagram 54, the harmonious co-operation of Black's pieces is again the decisive factor.

Black very clearly has the initiative, based on these factors:

1. Black has a threefold attack on White's weak Queen Bishop Pawn, which cannot be adequately defended.

2. Black's Rooks are both posted aggressively. One supports the Black threat just outlined; the other defends Black's advanced Queen Pawn.

Diagram 54 (*Black to play*)

BLACK

WHITE

3. Black's Knight has a powerful centralized position, and among other things, menaces White's Queen Bishop Pawn.

4. Black's Queen Pawn is a "passed" Pawn. (This means that it is free to advance because the hostile Pawns on either adjacent file are no longer free to capture it when it does so.) Such a Pawn has enormous dynamic power, as its possible advance involves serious dangers for White.

5. Black's Bishops are trained on White's King-side.

In certain situations, as will become clear very shortly, these Bishops can unleash considerable power.

6. Most of White's pieces are hemmed in. His Bishop at Queen Knight 1, for example, is blocked by its own King Pawn.

7. White's Knight has no access to the center and is exposed to the dangerous thrust . . . P–Q6.

8. White's Queen and Rooks have no scope to speak of, and are functioning at a trifling fraction of their power.

This analysis of the situation in Diagram 54 indicates that Black is ready for decisive action.

WHITE	BLACK
1 . . .	P–Q6!

This crushing move utilizes the stored-up power of Black's passed Queen Pawn.

White cannot reply 2 BxN, for then 2 . . . PxN! (attacking White's Queen), followed by 3 . . . BxB wins a piece for Black.

So White must move his attacked Knight; but if 2 N–B3, NxP; 3 BxB, P–Q7! and the double attack by Black's mighty passed Queen Pawn wins one of the White Rooks. So White retreats with a view to blocking the terrible Pawn.

| 2 | N–N1 | NxP |
| 3 | B–Q2 | Q–Q3! |

Black "unpins" his Knight by moving his Queen off the Queen Bishop file, so that he threatens . . . NxNP. But above all he threatens . . . QxKRP mate. The harmonious interaction of Black's forces is very finely worked out.

4   N–B3   . . .

White must stop the checkmate: he has no time to guard his menaced Pawn.

4 . . .   NxNP

White resigns, as his attacked Queen has no refuge. If White tries 5 B–N4, there follows 5 . . . NxQ; 6 BxQ, RxR and Black has won a Rook.

Summary—The harmonious co-operation of Black's forces enabled him to combine multiple threats to a winning conclusion. The fact that White's position was disjointed made Black's task that much easier.

WINNING TECHNIQUES

The study of middle game play up to this point has stressed broad principles and general ideas. But there are also specific winning methods that can be applied in all sorts of situations.

A little familiarity with these methods will increase a player's ability enormously: his eyes will be open to winning possibilities that he would never have noticed before. The opportunities for using these techniques turn up very often; consequently they give a clue to decisive continuations that are ordinarily overlooked by the average player.

The following treatment of winning techniques will consider the three types that are by far the most common: the pin, the Knight fork, the double attack.

THE PIN

The pin is an attack on a hostile unit which is shielding another hostile unit from attack. The pin is "absolute" when the shielded piece is the King, for then the pinned unit cannot move. The pin is "relative" when a piece other than the King is being shielded, for then the pinned unit can legally move—even though it may not be advisable to do so.

In Diagram 55 Black's Rook and Knight are pinned by the White Queen. The Rook cannot move at all, as it shields the Black King from attack; this is an "absolute" pin. The Black Knight can *legally* move, although that would involve the loss of Black's Queen; this is a "relative" pin.

Whenever a pin exists, it must be studied carefully to determine whether it can yield some decisive advantage. If the pinned piece is protected by a Pawn, the defender's position is likely to be fairly secure. But

if the pinned piece is not guarded by a Pawn, it has to
be protected by a piece.

Diagram 55

BLACK

WHITE

When the pinned unit has to be protected by a piece,
it is likely that the defender's resources can be stretched
to the breaking point. This is the case in the situation
of Diagram 56.

Pinning Demonstrated

Black's Knight at King Bishop 3 is pinned by White's
Queen Bishop and cannot be guarded by a Pawn. Here
is how White takes advantage of the weakness in
Black's game:

	WHITE	BLACK
1	B/R4xN!	PxB

Diagram 56 (*White to play*)

BLACK

WHITE

Or 1 . . . BxB; 2 PxP, PxP; 3 QxQ (removing the defender of the pinned Knight), QRxQ; 4 BxN and White has won the pinned piece.

	WHITE	BLACK
2	PxP	PxP
3	BxN	. . .

Note that this wins a piece by removing the two defenders of the Black Bishop on Queen 2.

	WHITE	BLACK
3	. . .	QxB
4	QxB	. . .

White has won a piece. Had Black's King Knight
Pawn been at King Knight 2 in the position of Diagram
56, this Pawn would have protected the pinned Black
Knight, relieving the Black Queen of the onerous task
of double protecting duty.

There are times when a pin can be profitably exploited in combination with other themes, such as double
attack (pages 127–130) or discovered check (pages
38–39). The latter is illustrated in Diagram 57.

Pin and Discovered Check

Diagram 57 (*White to play*)

BLACK

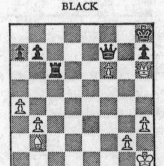

WHITE

Black is the Exchange ahead for two Pawns, so material is about equal. But White's King Bishop Pawn is
a far advanced passed Pawn which carries a potential

threat of advancing to the eighth rank and becoming a new Queen. Momentarily Black's Queen blocks the continued advance of the formidable Pawn. So White uses a startling method to blast away this blockade.

WHITE   BLACK

1   Q–B8ch!!   . . .

On the face of it this is a terrible blunder which loses the White Queen "for nothing." Actually this move is a sacrifice, as White expects to get worth-while compensation for his Queen.

1   . . .   QxQ

Now the blockade of the formidable passed Pawn is lifted and the formidable passed Pawn is free to advance, opening up a brusque discovered check by White's Bishop.

2   P–B7 dis ch   Q–N2
3   P–B8/Q mate!

The point is that White's new Queen is immune from capture *because Black's Queen is pinned.*

THE KNIGHT FORK

The Knight fork is one of the most common and most spectacular winning methods in chess. It fills the inexperienced player with dread because he is rarely on guard against the Knight's simultaneous attack in two different directions. When the Knight fork is made *with check*, as in Diagram 58, its peremptory effectiveness is greatly increased.

Diagram 58 (*Black to play*)

BLACK

WHITE

In Diagram 58 White's Knight forks the Black King and Queen *with check*. Black's Queen is lost because he has to move his King out of check.

In Diagram 59 a similar position is constructed by Black in a more complex situation.

At first sight it does not seem advisable for Black to play 1 . . . QxB; 2 QxQ, RxQ for after 3 RxR Black is the Exchange down. Yet this continuation *is* playable

Diagram 59 (*Black to play*)

BLACK

WHITE

for Black, as he has a devastating Knight fork at his disposal.

WHITE	BLACK
1 . . .	QxB!
2 QxQ	RxQ
3 RxR	N–B8ch

The point. Black's Knight forks White's King and Rook *with check,* forcing White's King to move; whereupon Black follows up with 4 . . . NxR. The result is that Black has won a piece.

DOUBLE ATTACK

Using a single unit to simultaneously attack two or more hostile units or to simultaneously attack in two or more directions is an integral part of powerful chess play. This explains why double attack is one of the most popular tactical motifs on the chessboard.

As a matter of fact, the Knight fork is a form of double attack. But the Queen, Rook, Bishop and Pawn can also engage in double attacks. Diagram 60 illustrates double attacks by Queen, Rook, and Bishop.

In Diagram 60 Black's Rook attacks White's Knight, Bishop, and Pawn.

Diagram 60 (*Black to play*)

BLACK

WHITE

White's Bishop attacks Black's Knight and Pawn.

White's Queen is attacking Black's Rook and Bishop and giving check as well.

In Diagram 61 White has a murderous double attack with a Pawn in combination with a Knight fork. This splendid example is utterly convincing in its blend of simplicity and ruthlessness.

Diagram 61 (*White to play*)

BLACK

WHITE

WHITE	BLACK
1 P–N6ch!	...

A Pawn fork. If Black does not capture the Pawn, he loses a Rook.

1 ...	KxP
2 N–B4ch	...

A decisive Knight fork with check. Black must move his King, allowing 3 NxQ.

Another way to proceed in Diagram 61 is for White to play 1 N–B4, attacking Black's Queen and also threatening the Pawn fork P–N6ch. This would leave Black helpless.

Diagram 62 offers impressive proof that the Queen, with its power of multiple attack, is the ideal piece for double attacks.

Diagram 62 (*White to play*)

BLACK

WHITE

WHITE	BLACK
1 Q–B5!	. . .

White attacks the *unprotected* Black Rook, but above all he threatens 2 QxRPch, K–B1; 3 Q–R8 mate. So Black must parry the mate threat (say by 1 . . . P–

N3), allowing White to play 2 QxRch with an easy win.

Any player who utilizes the simple techniques and principles outlined in this chapter can improve his middle game play enormously and prepare the basis for further rewarding study and improvement.

CHAPTER 6

The Decisive Phase:
Endgame Play

THE term "endgame" is self-explanatory. This is the final phase where all pending accounts are settled and all unfinished business is completed.

Some games are wound up in the middle game—or even in the opening—through some spectacular blunder that results in checkmate or a gain of material so substantial that the loser prefers to give up the ghost right then and there.

Normally, however, the forces are gradually pared down by successive exchanges to reach the rather simplified stage known as the endgame. The Queens in particular are likely to be gone from the board.

ENDGAME OBJECTIVES

Few players outside the expert class have a clear notion of what is involved in the endgame. Basically it deals with two problems:

1. How to exploit a material advantage that is sufficient to force checkmate.

2. How to transform an extra Pawn into a Queen.

The first problem is really basic; for a player who transforms a Pawn into a Queen can then proceed to force checkmate. The fundamental checkmating positions were shown in Diagrams 32-35. But the mechanics of forcing these checkmates are the most important aspect of endgame play.

EXPLOITING MATERIAL ADVANTAGE

Checkmate by the Queen

A typical situation of King and Queen against lone King is shown in Diagram 63.

Diagram 63 (*White to play*)

BLACK

WHITE

The checkmating procedure is as follows:

1. The lone King must be driven to the side of the board.

2. King and Queen then co-operate to force checkmate.

WHITE	BLACK
1 Q–Q5	K–K2
2 K–N5	K–K1

Black's King has been forced to the side.

3 K–B6   K–B1

Now White can play 4 Q–B7 mate (Diagram 32) or 4 Q–R8 mate or 4 Q–Q8 mate. Diagram 64 shows the position after 4 Q–Q8 mate.

Diagram 64 (*Black is checkmated*)

BLACK

WHITE

Diagram 65 (*Black to play*)

BLACK

WHITE

Checkmate by the Rook

The checkmate with the Rook is slightly more difficult, because the Rook lacks the diagonal powers of the Queen. The procedure is similar:

1. The lone King must be driven to the side of the board.

2. King and Rook then co-operate to force checkmate.

WHITE	BLACK
1 ...	K–Q4
2 K–B3	K–Q5
3 K–B2	...

If 3 K–B4, R–KB8ch forcing White's King toward the side.

3	. . .	R–K6
4	K–B1	K–Q6
5	K–B2	K–Q7
6	K–N2	K–K7
7	K–N1	K–B6
8	K–R2	R–K1
9	K–N1	R–KR1
10	K–B1	R–R8 mate

The checkmate position appears in Diagram 66.

Diagram 66 (*White is checkmated*)

BLACK

WHITE

Checkmate by the Two Bishops

This checkmate is still harder, requiring effective co-operation among the checkmating pieces. The procedure is as follows:

1. The lone King must be driven to the side of the board.

2. The lone King must be forced into a corner.

3. King and Bishops then co-operate to force checkmate.

Diagram 67 (*White to play*)

BLACK

WHITE

WHITE	BLACK
1 B–B5!	K–R5

Black's King has been forced to the side of the board.

2	B–B4!	K–R4
3	K–B6	K–R5
4	B–Q5	K–R4
5	B–N3!	K–R3

Black's King is being driven into a corner.

6	B–N4!	K–R2
7	K–B7!	K–R3
8	B–B4ch	K–R2
9	B–B5ch	K–R1
10	B–Q5 mate	

Diagram 68 (*Black is checkmated*)

BLACK

WHITE

Checkmate by Bishop and Knight

This is the hardest of all the basic checkmates. The procedure is as follows:

1. The lone King must be driven to the side of the board.

2. The lone King must be forced into a corner square of the same color as those the Bishop travels on.

3. King, Bishop and Knight then co-operate to force checkmate.

Given the situation in Diagram 69, White's King can only be checkmated on a white corner square.

Diagram 69 (*Black to play*)

BLACK

WHITE

The fact that White's King is already on a side row facilitates the checkmating process.

	WHITE	BLACK
1	...	N–B5
2	K–B1	B–Q8
3	K–K1	B–N5
4	K–B1	B–K7ch!

Forcing White's King toward the corner square, for if 5 K–K1?, N–Q6 mate (or 5 ... N–N7 mate).

	WHITE	BLACK
5	K–N1	K–B6
6	K–R2	K–B7
7	K–R1	B–B8!
8	K–R2	N–K7

Diagram 70 (*White is checkmated*)

BLACK

WHITE

	9	K–R1	N–Q5
	10	K–R2	N–B6ch
	11	K–R1	B–N7 mate

The final checkmate position appears in Diagram 70.

THE POWER OF PAWN PROMOTION

It is one of the marks of a first-class chessplayer to realize that *most endgames center about Pawn promotion or the threat of Pawn promotion*. The play from Diagram 71 is a good example.

Diagram 71 (*White to play*)

BLACK

WHITE

It is obvious that White's Queen, attacked by Black's Bishop Pawn, must move. But instead of retreating the

Queen, White chooses an astounding alternative, based on these factors:

1. White's Queen Bishop Pawn is a passed Pawn.

2. Its progress to the queening square is blockaded by Black's Queen.

3. Black's Queen also has the task of guarding his Rook.

4. By sacrificing his Queen for the Black Rook, White can force the removal of Black's blockading Queen.

WHITE	BLACK
1 QxR!	QxQ
2 P–B7	Resigns

No matter how Black plays, he will be left a Rook down. And, as he is helpless against the coming P–B8/Q, he rightly gives up the struggle.

Control the Queening Square

Diagram 72 illustrates still another important facet of Pawn promotion. By gaining control of the prospective queening square, it is often possible to win substantial material that must be surrendered by the opponent to get rid of the newly promoted Queen.

Although material is *quantitatively* even here, there is a great deal of difference *qualitatively*.

Black's Queen Bishop Pawn, though passed, is still

on its original square. Its queening possibilities, considered with ruthless realism, are nonexistent.

On the other hand, White's passed Queen Rook Pawn *has advanced to the seventh rank and is on the point of queening.*

The qualitative distinction is so huge that White can force a direct win.

Diagram 72 (*White to play*)

BLACK

WHITE

WHITE	BLACK
1 Q–N8!	Resigns

Further play by Black would be futile.

White's Queen move *controls the queening square,* ensuring the immediate promotion P–R8/Q. No matter how Black plays, he will be left a whole Queen down.

This theme is of such great practical value and it is

so generally neglected that it deserves another illustration.

In Diagram 73 the win hangs by a hair. *If it were Black's turn to play*, he could continue with 1 . . . K–K2 or 1 . . . K–K3 or 1 . . . R–Q1, confiscating White's dangerous passed Queen Pawn and then winning the game because of his advantage of the Exchange (page 66).

But, as matters stand, it is White's turn to play—and this makes all the difference.

For, if White plays correctly, he can control the queening square of his far-advanced passed Pawn.

Diagram 73 (*White to play*)

BLACK

WHITE

WHITE	BLACK
1 B–R4!	. . .

This move controls the queening square.

White's next move will be 2 P–Q8/Q, forcing Black to give up his Rook for the new Queen. Then 3 BxR will leave White a Bishop to the good, with an easy win in due course.

These examples of the power of a far-advanced passed Pawn should be studied with great care. Pawn promotion can win many games.

King and Pawn Endings

These basic endings are useful to know, as they turn up repeatedly in practical play. A knowledge of these fundamental positions will often spell the difference between a win and a draw.

The situation shown in Diagram 74 is of great prac-

Diagram 74 (*White to play*)

BLACK

WHITE

tical value, since conceivably it can always turn up, after many exchanges, in any game where a player is a Pawn ahead. In fact, in contests between experts, a player with that advantage will deliberately steer for an ending in which only Kings and Pawns are left on the board.

As far as the materially weaker opponent is concerned, the mere possibility of such an ending is one of the most potent threats in chess.

White's objective is to control the queening square (Queen 8) with his King. To do this, he must bring his King to King 7 or Queen Bishop 7. Once the plan succeeds, the queening of the Pawn is assured.

WHITE	BLACK
1 K–Q6!	. . .

Placing the White King so that the Kings face each other *at the opponent's turn to move* results in "having the Opposition": Black's King must give way.

1 . . .	K–K1

If 1 . . . K–B1, White wins in similar fashion with 2 K–K7.

2 K–B7	. . .

Now White can force the queening of the Pawn. For example:

2 . . .	K–K2

3	P–Q6ch	K–K1
4	P–Q7ch	K moves
5	P–Q8/Q	. . .

And White will soon force checkmate.

In Diagram 74, White has still another way to win:

WHITE	BLACK
1 K–K6	K–K1

Black momentarily has the Opposition, but White can get it back by advancing his Pawn.

| 2 | P–Q6! | . . . |

Now White has the Opposition. Black's King must give way.

| 2 | . . . | K–Q1 |
| 3 | P–Q7 | . . . |

When White's King is on the sixth rank and his Pawn advances to the seventh rank *without giving check*, he wins the ending.

If the Pawn gives check on the seventh rank, the game will end in a draw, despite the Pawn advantage. This will be explained later on.

| 3 | . . . | K–B2 |

Unfortunately for Black, he must allow White to play K–K7.

4 K–K7 ...

This wins, as Black is helpless against the coming 5 P–Q8/Q.

As a reminder that unexpected tactical fireworks have their place in the endgame too, the position in Diagram 75 can be won by White despite the fact that material is perfectly even.

In such positions, where both players are racing to queen a Pawn, the player who queens first may sometimes have a decisive advantage. This is the case in Diagram 75.

Diagram 75 (*White to play*)

BLACK

WHITE

WHITE	BLACK
1 P–R4	P–N4
2 P–R5	P–N5

    3 P–R6   P–N6
    4 P–R7   P–N7
    5 P–R8/Q   P–N8/Q

Now both players have new Queens—but White moves first.

    6 Q–KB8ch   K–N4
    7 Q–KN8ch ...

This check—something to watch for in such endings—wins Black's Queen, and the game.

Rook and Pawn Endings

These endings (with a King and Rook apiece and one or more Pawns on the board) are very common. The most important basic ending in this category is the one shown in Diagram 76.

In the position of Diagram 76, White wants to queen his Pawn, which has already reached the seventh rank. In order to promote the Pawn, he must get his King out of the way. But in the present situation he cannot move his King. He therefore drives Black's King away.

        WHITE   BLACK
    1   R–Q1ch   K–B2

Now it is still too soon for White to move his King: 2 K–K7, R–K7ch; 3 K–B6, R–KB7ch; 4 K–K6, R–K7 ch; 5 K–Q5, R–KB7; 6 K–K6, R–K7ch and White can make no headway.

Diagram 76 (*White to play*)

BLACK

WHITE

2 R–Q4!   . . .

The winning idea. White will now bring his King out and eventually escape from a rain of checks by interposing his Rook at the right moment:

2	. . .	R–N7
3	K–K7	R–K7ch
4	K–B6	R–KB7ch
5	K–N6	R–KN7ch
6	K–B5	R–KB7ch
7	R–KB4!	. . .

This ends the checks and leaves Black helpless against the coming queening of White's Pawn.

Diagram 77 illustrates a neat tactical trick which has proved useful in more than one Rook and Pawn ending.

Diagram 77 (*White to play*)

BLACK

WHITE

In the position of Diagram 77, White of course wants to queen his far-advanced Pawn. In order to do so, he must move his Rook. But if he moves his Rook, he loses his Pawn. Here is how he solves the difficulty.

WHITE	BLACK
1 R–KR8!	...

The only move to win.

1 ...	RxP

Black has no choice, as the Pawn threatens to queen.

2 R–R7ch . . .

This stratagem wins the Rook—by the same device used in Diagram 75—after which White can deliver checkmate.

USEFUL DRAWING METHODS

There are many endgame situations where a draw is the best one can hope for. In such cases, it is useful to be familiar with standard drawing patterns. The theme is interestingly illustrated in Diagram 78. (The same situation was discussed in a different context on page 146.)

Diagram 78 (*White to play*)

BLACK

WHITE

If White plays the wrong move, Black can draw by best play, despite his material disadvantage.

WHITE   BLACK

1 P–Q6?   ...

With this move White throws away the win.

1 ...   K–Q2!

This move draws. (Note that 1 . . . K–K1? loses, as White replies 2 K–K6 with the winning position described on page 147.)

2 K–Q5   K–Q1!

The only move to draw, for if 2 . . . K–B1; 3 K–B6, or if 2 . . . K–K1; 3 K–K6, and in either case White's King gets control of the Pawn's queening square.

3 K–K6   K–K1!

Black has the Opposition.

4 P–Q7ch   ...

On page 147 it was stated that if the Pawn gives check on the seventh rank in this situation, the game is a draw. This is the reason:

4 ...   K–Q1

Now White has only one move to avoid losing his Pawn.

5 K–Q6   ...

Stalemate! The game is a draw.

Another useful drawing resource is shown in Diagram 79.

Diagram 79 (White to play)

BLACK

WHITE

The standard winning procedure shown in Diagram 74 does not apply in the case of the Rook Pawn. If Black plays properly, he will always draw against the Rook Pawn. The reason becomes clear on studying the play from Diagram 79.

WHITE	BLACK
1 K–R6	. . .

White takes the Opposition—but in this exceptional position it is of no avail.

1 . . .	K–N1

In the analogous position arising from Diagram 74, White now played a forward diagonal move with his King (K–K7), which gave him control of the queening square.

But here, since *White's King is already at the edge of the board,* he cannot make a similar King move. Consequently, he cannot control the queening squares. This explains why the Rook Pawn cannot win.

2	K–N6	K–R1
3	P–R6	K–N1
4	P–R7ch	K–R1
5	K–R6	. . .

Black is stalemated. The game is a draw.

Drawing with Bishops on Opposite Colors

Another useful drawing method which often avoids loss turns up in Bishop and Pawn endings. These are endgames with Pawns in which each side has a King and Bishop. Such a situation is shown in Diagram 80.

Diagram 80 (*Black to play*)

BLACK

WHITE

Incredible as it may seem, Black's material advantage in the position of Diagram 80 is quite worthless. Although he is two Pawns ahead, he has no way of making progress.

This often happens when the Bishops move on *opposite colors*. White's Bishop is limited to the white squares, while Black's Bishop can move only on black squares. Thus Black has no control over the white squares.

This is why Black can make no progress, and why the position is a draw despite Black's extra Pawns. White's King can not be driven off his blockading position at King 2 as long as White keeps his Bishop on the long diagonal from King Rook 1 to Queen Rook 8.

The handful of examples in this chapter is only a tiny fragment of the vast repertoire of endgame play. Nevertheless, these endings will prove of great practical value.

Above all, the student will do well to concentrate on the theme of queening which is at the heart of almost every endgame. Keeping this theme constantly in mind is the first and perhaps the most important step in learning to play endings successfully.

CHAPTER 7

Conclusion

IN this book you have learned all you need to know about the basic rules of chess—how each of the chessmen moves, and how games are won, and drawn. You have also learned the relative values of all the forces; you now know how to read chess notation and diagrams. You are familiar with the methods of bringing about the basic checkmates.

You have acquired the fundamentals of good opening play, and you have been shown the kinds of mistakes that must be avoided in the opening. You know the characteristics of the best openings and the moves which distinguish them.

As for the middle game, you have studied the basic principles which will give you a good position, and you have learned the most valuable tactical tricks which will enable you to win material.

In the endgame chapter you observed the importance of the Pawn promotion motif, and saw how it applies to various kinds of endgames. Finally, you studied a number of valuable drawing methods that will often stave off disaster in seemingly lost positions.

Where do you go from here? Above all, you need more practice and experience. Seek opportunities for play; the more you play, the better you will be able to apply what you have already learned.

Where you have a choice of opponents, seek out the ones who are on your level—or even a little better. If they are much stronger players than you, you will become discouraged or shrink into a timid style which is harmful to your development as a chessplayer. However, if your opponents are only slightly better than you, you will have a direct stimulus to improve just enough to be able to hold your own with them.

Such a goal, which is rewarding and at the same time well within the scope of your abilities, will add zest to your chess play. It will encourage you to read more chess books, which will in turn be the source of further enjoyment and further improvement. In both respects chess offers almost limitless horizons. It is a lifetime hobby which will afford you ever greater pleasure and will always offer something new to learn, to experience, and to enjoy.

To complete this survey of what you need to know about chess, we must familiarize ourselves with the rules that govern the physical execution of a move. In the absence of such rules, unpleasant arguments sometimes arise, and it is a good idea to be able to refer to a recognized authority.

The following summary is based on the official rules of the International Chess Federation.

WHEN IS A MOVE COMPLETED?

Once a player has moved a chessman to an empty square and taken his hand off it, the move is completed and cannot be retracted. Note that you can invoke the following rules if there has been a prior agreement to observe them.

When making a capture, the move is complete and cannot be retracted once a player has removed the captured chessman from the board and has placed the capturing chessman on its new square and taken his hand off it.

In castling, the player moves the King first. After making the King move, he has not completed castling until he has moved the Rook as well, and taken his hand off it. However, even though castling is not completed after the King is moved, the player can make no other move but castling once he has moved the King and taken his hand off it.

In promoting a Pawn, the move is not completed when the player has advanced the Pawn to the eighth rank and has taken his hand off it. However, he no longer has the right to move the Pawn elsewhere.

In any event, the Pawn promotion is completed when the player has advanced the Pawn to the eighth rank, removed it from the board, replaced it with the new piece of his choice, and taken his hand off the new piece.

TOUCHING A CHESSMAN

A player can adjust the position of any chessman by first announcing his intention to do so.

If the player, without making such announcement, touches a chessman or several chessmen, he must move or capture the first chessman touched which can move or capture. If either is impossible, there is no penalty. Likewise there is no penalty if there has been no prior understanding that this rule will apply.

ILLEGAL POSITIONS

If you discover during the course of a game that an illegal move has been made at some point, you must reconstruct the position as it was just before the illegal move was made. If it is impossible to reconstruct the position, then the game must be canceled and a new game started.

Index